KABBALAH MADE EASY

*Ancient mystical wisdom
decoded for modern life*

Barrie Dolnick

PIATKUS

First published in the US in 2005 by
New American Library, a division of Penguin Group (USA) Inc.

First published in Great Britain in 2006 by
Piatkus Books Ltd
5 Windmill Street, London W1T 2JA
email: info@piatkus.co.uk

The moral right of the author has been asserted

A catalogue record for this book is available from the British Library

ISBN 0 7499 2689 9

This book has been printed on paper manufactured with respect for the
environment using wood from managed sustainable resources

Designed by Jennifer Ann Dadio

Data manipulation by Phoenix Photosetting, Chatham, Kent
Printed and bound in Great Britain by
Mackays Ltd, Chatham, Kent

KABBALAH MADE EASY

Also by Barrie Dolnick

ASTROBABE

DREAMBABE

KARMABABE

Acknowledgments

Eternal thanks to my husband, Gero, and daughter, Elisabeth, for ignoring my muttering.

Thanks to my mother, Sandy Dolnick, and my sisters, Randy, Amy, and Carol, who helped recall some of the choice moments of religious education, and to my brothers-in-law, John and Sean, for not taking any notice of us.

Thanks to Sy and Bunny Dolnick, who I hope will be relieved to see that the lineage is still alive.

Thanks to the girlfriends, Patty Brundage, Cheryl Callan, Christine Chiocchio, Julia Condon, Sheila Davidson, Valerie de LaValette Loo, Shelly Fremont,

Joelle O'Reilly-Hyland, and Amy State, for their support and humor.

Many thanks to new friends Rabbi James Ponet and Elana Ponet for not making me feel totally ignorant.

And thanks to old friends Sandi Dorman and Susan Strong, who reminded me of my roots.

Contents

Preface

What's all this you've been hearing about the Kabbalah? If you're wondering what Madonna and Britney and all those other celebrities are up to with their little red bracelets and parties in a Kabbalah center, this book is for you. Is it a secret society? A Jewish mystical cult? Can anyone learn about it? You're not alone if you're curious. For any questions you have about Kabbalah, read on. You can learn about Kabbalah without leaving your house and you don't have to join anything.

Kabbalah is a mystical pathway open to anyone who cares to explore and expand herself.

Kabbalah Made Easy might sound like a fun, easy fling with some cool, faddish new hobby, but it's more than that. Sure, mystical teachings can be fun, but Kabbalah has been around too long to qualify as a fad. Kabbalah is an ancient body of knowledge, a very complex model of what/who God is, who you are, and most important, who you can be.

Who Can Resist? Not Me!

I have studied metaphysics and spiritual topics for over twenty years, so writing about the Kabbalah seemed a natural undertaking. Besides, I was brought up Jewish, and Kabbalah is a Jewish mystical practice, after all. True, I hadn't been observant in years and never felt a spiritual kinship with my ancestral religion. But here was the chance to find it.

Luckily, Kabbalah doesn't demand that you know much about Judaism. I remembered a bit of the Hebrew alphabet and a few Bible stories, but that's all. Studying the Kabbalah, or at least reading many books about the Kabbalah in order to write about it, I realized it's not *about* religious observation. They don't teach Kabbalah in Sunday school!

Reading the various authors and scholars who are entrenched in Kabbalah is like sitting in the middle of an ancient library listening to men arguing and shushing each other. I don't know if it's cultural or just human nature, but no one agrees on who is qualified to learn Kabbalah and who is qualified to teach it. Some authors on Kabbalah go so far as to put down the views of others. Experts on Kabbalah are a high-spirited group who do not give way to one view or one leader. So in that spirit, I'm throwing in my two shekels and offering you a look at Kabbalah from an outsider's perspective. Granted, I'm an outsider who has a head start in interpreting metaphysical and spiritual beliefs.

There are many scholars, teachers, and critics of Kabbalah, and I quickly learned that they will tell you conflicting "truths" at every step of the process. This is almost the first lesson of Kabbalah. Many Kabbalists promise that you'll learn exactly why you are here and the exact number of steps it will take you to get to God. Others will tell you that you have to simply open yourself to the energy of the Zohar (the central text of the Kabbalah) and it will come to you. All too often they promise to reveal the indisputable truth, a promise impossible to deliver.

The one thing everyone agrees on is that studying the Kabbalah can improve your life and make you a better person.

Having written this book, I can tell you that Kabbalah has definitely challenged me, inspired me, and made me more aware of my actions and motivations. Lessons from the Kabbalah have permeated my daily life.

As you read through these basic lessons in Kabbalah, remember to pause, question, and digest. Kabbalah is a process, not a recipe book that outlines exact rules. Some of the basic tenets of Kabbalah may not seem relevant or even make sense to you right away. Take time, revisit, let the wisdom penetrate, then illuminate.

Kabbalah has many layers. As you peel each one away, you open further and further to Divine light, and to sharing with others. Sharing light brings you closer to the spirit of the Creator. So read on, open to the knowledge, and enlighten up.

Getting Started with Kabbalah

Kabbalah Is Complex

I have a friend who is a well-known author and expert on the Kabbalah. He laughed when I told him I was writing a book called *Kabbalah Made Easy*.

"That's going to be interesting. I've been studying it for years. It's an amorphous body of work."

Can you really learn the keys to Kabbalah just by reading a book? Well, it's a good start.

There are stacks and piles and archives of information, opinions, and assertions about Kabbalah and there isn't a single book or expert who knows it all or who has every element contained in perfect order.

The first and most important lesson you can learn about the Kabbalah is that there really is no single answer to any one question. Confusing? Yes. Difficult to understand? It can be. But don't give up here. You'll decide on the answers that work for you.

Here's a great example. Even the name "Kabbalah," an English transliteration of an ancient Aramaic word, has no "right" spelling. You'll see "Kabbalah," "Kaballah," "Qabala," "Cabala," and so on. Basically, any three syllables that connect to sound like *Kah-bah-lah* will do. Some people put the accent on the second syllable *(Kah-BAH-lah)* and others give even stress to each syllable. For this book, we'll use the spelling now popularized by the Kabbalah centers that have attracted so many celebrity followers and so much press attention.

There is an old saying that if you have one problem and ask two Jews to solve it, you'll end up with at least three answers.

What does the word "Kabbalah" mean? In simple terms, "Kabbalah" means "to receive," but of course, there's more to it. A subtler translation of the word "Kabbalah" is really "to receive in order to share," so it's not a "take this—it's yours to keep" type of receivership. Within this context, "Kabbalah" is also translated to mean "tradition." Kabbalah is received from the previous generation and eventually shared with the next.

In a greater sense, Kabbalah means you can receive all that you want in the universe—wisdom, abundance, love—and that once you have it, you share it with others. It's really a cycle—what you get, you give; then you get more, you give more, and so it goes. It's fine to be rich as long as you give back. It's great to be wise as long as you teach others. It's wonderful to be loved as long as you share your love, too.

For those of you who have studied other religions or spiritual practices, Kabbalah is going to sound very familiar. The names are different, the approach might seem different, but the basic teachings, the basic principles, are all heading to the same place. All roads lead to (or unite us with) Infinite Spirit. In Kabbalah this energy is most often called the Creator. Yet again, there's no right answer to what this infinite source is called. You can call it whatever you like—God, spirit, energy. It is nameless because it is inconceivable. God isn't an old man sitting up on a cloud fiddling with your future. In Kabbalah, the Creator is the source of all that is and that will be. If you read books about Kabbalah, you're going to see that the Creator is inevitably referred to as "he," but don't despair. God is not allied with one sex and won't be defined as "he" in this book.

You don't have to be Jewish to study Kabbalah. I have to admit, if you have a working knowledge of Hebrew, it helps. It also helps to be familiar with Old Testament stories. But it's *not* necessary.

Kabbalah is not a religion; it is a spiritual practice. It is a pathway, an energy, a connection. If you plug into it by studying, practicing, and applying it to your life, you are going to benefit. But if you simply want to learn what it's about, your knowledge and experience in life will grow as a result. There is no downside. There is no commitment. You can't help but enrich your mind, body, and soul simply by knowing more about Kabbalah.

The Roots of Kabbalah

Not surprisingly, there is more than one theory about where Kabbalah was born. The most traditional, even mythical theory is that Abraham was given the Kabbalah's first teachings by God (the Creator). Abraham's followers, the ancient people of Israel, received further knowledge of the Kabbalah (from prophets, angels, sages) and passed it along through the spoken word. Some scholars assert that the first written lessons of the Kabbalah were the Ten Commandments. For many centuries, this sacred, mystical knowledge was passed down through generations, and some who studied with great discipline and isolation were said to be visited by prophets. Scholars throughout the ages studied the Kabbalah—these scholars were rabbis (the word "rabbi" means "teacher"). From the time of Jesus through the Middle Ages, many different rabbis "received and shared" Kabbalistic information.

At some point, someone decided to record the stories and teachings of Kabbalah. These exist today in a multivolume book called the Zohar *(Zoe-harr)*, or the Book of Radiance. Many layers of knowledge and teachings make up this vast work, and people have spent their lives reading and studying its stories. Unfortunately, the Zohar isn't an instruction manual with all the secrets of Kabbalah neatly spelled out. It's a meandering compilation of stories and instructions, much like the Bible.

The origins of the Zohar are not clear—and this

makes for lively debate among Kabbalistic scholars. Some say it was written in about A.D. 200 by a rabbi and his son who hid in a cave for thirteen years while the Romans were trying to annihilate the Jews. Other scholars attribute the Zohar to Moses de León, a scholar who lived in thirteenth-century Europe. Suffice it to say that the Zohar is a dynamic piece of spiritual literature. The Zohar is considered sacred, Divine. It is the central text of Kabbalah.

If you're wondering why you shouldn't just pick up a copy of the Zohar instead of this book, it's because the Zohar is very, very long, very expensive, and not what you'd call easy reading. Scholars spend a lifetime studying the Zohar in its original Aramaic, dissecting every sentence in order to purify its meaning. That makes translation particularly difficult and time-consuming. (If you're very interested, keep an eye out for the new translation of the Zohar called the Pritzker Edition. At the time of this publication, only one volume of a projected ten is available.) Of course, some people believe that just skimming your fingers across the printed page of Aramaic text will bring Divine light and energy to you. That's a pretty wide range for experiencing the Zohar—from word-by-word interpretation to simply touching the page. Which way appeals to you?

The teachings in the Zohar are said to be intricate and indirect. I don't know firsthand, of course, not being fluent in Aramaic. But just because the text was "given" to rabbis and was written in the Hebrew alphabet (that's what Aramaic looks like) doesn't make it exclusive to those who read those languages. There are many thoughtful books that put forth its basic teachings and stories in translated excerpts. Ultimately, the Zohar presents essential, solid metaphysical principles that apply to *everyone* on this planet.

Can Anyone Study Kabbalah?

There are different opinions about who is "allowed" to study the Kabbalah.

Here are the answers to the question: Can *anyone* study the Kabbalah?

Answer One: No

If you're not male, over forty, married with at least three kids, educated in basic Jewish teachings, and living in Israel, you're not permitted. That's a traditional, some say antiquated, approach to Kabbalah study.

Answer Two: Maybe

Are you prepared to take this seriously and devote
yourself to the depth and demands of the Kabbalah?
Most Kabbalists teach only serious students and screen
their applicants for devotion. Some teachers don't ask
for money—they just want your commitment.

Answer Three: Yes

The currently popularized form of Kabbalah wel-
comes anyone who is interested to share in basic
knowledge and principles. Here's where *we* fit in. You
don't have to be Jewish, live in Israel, or even commit
to a long-term study program. You may find that
you like studying the Kabbalah and jump to the next
level, but you don't have to. Kabbalah centers as
well as informal study groups and nontraditional
teachers are available for you to explore the mysteries
of the Kabbalah without committing yourself to years
of study.

The Secrets of Kabbalah

From the beginning of my own studies in spirituality
and metaphysics, I'd heard that the Kabbalah was a

"secret" mystical tradition. To be fair, I'd also heard this about the Masons, the Knights Templars, and several other spiritual societies. Just saying the word "secret" makes the subject all the more attractive, doesn't it?

Historically, there were several reasons to keep Kabbalah secret. First, some of the Kabbalah's teachings seem to contradict Jewish doctrine. There are still some rabbinic scholars who object to the study of Kabbalah and insist that it is against Jewish law. Some information in the Kabbalah does indeed seem more pagan than Jewish, including numerology, astrology, and theories of reincarnation.

Second, those in power have historically tended to try to reserve certain fields of knowledge for themselves. They also prefer to share it only with others like them. Hence the rules about being an over-forty married father of three. The knowledge of Kabbalah was reserved for serious scholars—all of whom were men—who were firmly established in the community.

Kabbalistic knowledge has also always been considered very powerful, so much so that scholars didn't want newcomers to be overwhelmed by this Divine information. Ancient Kabbalists held their teachings closely so that amateurs wouldn't get carried away,

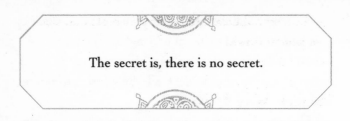

> The secret is, there is no secret.

and so power would be kept out of the wrong hands. Famous historical figures, such as Renaissance humanist Pico della Mirandola, learned Kabbalah in order to be privy to this perceived power.

Historically, only men learned and interpreted the Kabbalah. It's unclear why Kabbalah (and Judaism) grew so one-sidedly masculine.

It wasn't always that way. Author and Kabbalah expert Judy Greenfeld shares her take on women's influence:

> "Sarah was considered a very special Prophetess before embarking on her journey to become a Jewish people with Abraham. The Torah tells us that God told Abraham, "Listen to the voice of Sarah!" The "voice" is her wisdom and prophecy and gift. So the wisdom that we — people of spirit and God — are all coming from is the same source."

In true Kabbalah, the light we create and share is not gender biased.

Which Way Is Right?

Oy vey (this means "Oh, pain!").

Here's the thing: no one can tell you "the Truth." You have to use your own heart and soul to connect to truth.

There are people who will try to tell you that only one way is the true way of God. There are those who will tell you that Kabbalah is the only way to God. You'll also hear this from fundamentalists in Christianity, Islam, Hinduism—you name it. Come on, no person can say what is God's truth! Just by virtue of being human, we're exempt from seeing the truth about God. We can study, learn, experience, and believe. We can have faith and feel God's love. But you have to *sense* what is meaningful for you. Commit wholeheartedly or cherry-pick from all religions and spiritual practices. Decide for yourself. It's not that hard—just follow your heart.

Having studied many ancient philosophies and cultures, I'm of the opinion that they're all the same at their core. If you strip away the stories, the names, and the rituals, you'll find the basic teachings are similar: connection, love, sharing, forgiveness, finding a way to spirit—these are central to virtually all spiritual practices.

The differences among spiritual practices stem from the cultures where they originated and the moment in time they were born. Kabbalah happens to have been born with Abraham (or so the story goes) and carries with it a strong influence of Judaism and Jewish culture.

Light, Not Wisdom

Ultimately, the benefits of studying and practicing Kabbalah don't revolve around learning new ideas or committing rules to memory. Kabbalah is a path to light.

Light is a common thread in all spiritual practice—not just Kabbalah.

Light = Enlightenment =
Illumination = Spiritual Alignment

Receiving light does not mean having a lightbulb go off cartoonishly over your head. Light is actually a nonphysical essence that we perceive in different ways. Some feel light glowing from the core of their heart or essence. Others feel lightness in their whole being—like weightlessness. Still others feel a light from the heavens pouring down through their body.

Light illuminates your soul and encourages you to share with others. Your light can light the way for someone who is in the dark.

Here's an example. Let's say you're learning to open to your compassion, a lesson we'll approach later in the book. Compassion is a big energy, one that comes from the heart and helps you connect to others without effort. You're at work, thinking how much you'd rather be somewhere else. One of your coworkers looks tired and asks if you'll cover for her. You're fed up because it seems like this girl is always trying to get out of work. You're about to refuse, but you remember your focus on compassion. You don't have anything to do. To deny her request is just hostile. You take a deep breath and find your heart energy. You relax and tell her it's okay.

The next day the same girl comes to you and thanks you with a small gift of flowers. You find out from someone else that she's been going to the hospital to visit her father as he struggles with some difficult illness. This coworker has never told you anything about her father, nor has she given an excuse to leave work.

Your compassion eased her pain. Your choice to put your annoyance aside gave her more time to cope. You shared your light. Score one for you.

Sharing light is very often about putting aside your own wants and needs. Sharing your light reaches beyond discomfort or aggravation and creates space for healing. What you don't see is how your light illuminates more than a single moment in life. Giving light creates more possibilities for others to do the same. That girl will more than likely share her time with others when she's able.

The other side, of course, is being able to take light when you need it. This is possibly a more difficult lesson. It requires you to be able to take in what others might offer you, to open yourself to light, forgiveness, love, patience. In order to do that, you have to "get over yourself." You have to let yourself be lifted when you're down. Pride, ego, and fear of humiliation can easily stand in the way. Asking for light is sometimes more difficult than giving it, because it can feel like an admission that you're not okay.

You'll find a natural equilibrium between giving and receiving. It's all in the balance. Take in light; give out light. The cycle is sacred, healing, and blessed.

What's Ahead

Having read Kabbalistic texts and interviewed scholars, I know how hard it is to explain the Kabbalah in simple terms. Not one to turn away from a challenge and, of course, being willing to share the light, I'm going to attempt to lay out the basics for you.

Our first consideration for understanding Kabbalah is to get an inkling of the great Creator and Creation. It's not enough to accept that there's a God or that God made the world. Kabbalah has very specific ideas about the Creator and Creation. It all comes back to the Beginning.

After the Beginning, we'll move to the Tree of Life. This is probably the most famous icon of Kabbalah. The Tree of Life offers a graphic guide to the Creator's energy and how we all got to be here. Many modern healers and voices of spirituality use the Tree of Life as a basis for teachings, meditations, and exercises. Kabbalists consider the Tree both sacred and complex, not something to be used or studied lightly. You'll no doubt find the Tree of Life interesting, complicated, and enlightening.

Since the roots of Kabbalah are firmly planted in the ancient language of Aramaic and now in Hebrew, we're going to throw around some exotic words and references. It can be confusing, but it is necessary, because Kabbalists believe in the power of numbers and how they correspond to the Hebrew alphabet. So we'll cover the Hebrew alphabet and some approaches to numerical meanings. It's not unlike modern numerology, but again, as in every aspect of Kabbalah, interpretation and use vary.

After we've explored the three basic keys of the Creator/Creation, the Tree of Life, and the significance of numbers and letters, we'll move on to angels, evil, and the soul's journey. Then we'll get a taste of how Kabbalists use these concepts to examine relationships between them. Finally, we'll look at some very real applications to your daily life. The only way to progress spiritually within the context of Kabbalah is to remember and live by its principles (not rules!). As you make your way through your life with more light, you move along on the path to joy.

Getting Started

Keep your mind as open as possible. If you're not Jewish or have had little exposure to Judaism, you might find this journey exotic and strange. Even if you are Jewish, you'll find that Kabbalah isn't your Sunday school version of the Torah.

Be patient. It's not a snap to understand Kabbalah. For thousands of years people have argued over every single word, and questioned every source, of the Kabbalah. It's not an instruction manual.

Take what you can from it. If nothing else, remember "to receive in order to share." If you walk away right now with just that, you're doing fine. If you want a taste of how Kabbalists open to this spiritual state, read on.

According to Kabbalah, the purpose of life is joy. And so the journey begins.

Creation

Start at the Beginning

"In the beginning, God created heaven and earth."
You've heard this first line of the Old Testament
before.

Okay, but what was God up to before then?

As children, many of us wondered what was in the
universe before that important day God got busy.
Kids who ask that question often get a dismissive answer like "You don't need to worry about that."

Well, that's where Kabbalists start to study. Yes,
it's time to comprehend the incomprehensible. Kab-

balists claim they have configured the structure of the universe/Creator (in rough conceptual terms) and how the energy of Creation came to be. It's the foundation of Kabbalah.

What Came Before the Beginning

Even before the universe, there existed the Creator. Even if there was only a great void of space — an infinite vacuum, endless nothingness — that's the Creator. The Creator is not a king who sits on a throne up in heaven and passes judgment. The Creator is an energy that has no gender, no physical description, no beginning, and no end. All and nothing. The Creator has no official name and really defies definition. It might seem easier to say what the Creator is NOT than what the Creator is, since the Creator is EVERYTHING AND NOTHING.

Scientists have calculated that Earth wasn't the first planet ever created, and there are stars much older than our Sun. But science won't try to tell us what came before the stars, or what came before whatever came before the stars (follow me?). What was there before the big bang? You can get fancy and bring up black holes, faraway galaxies, and exploding stars, or throw around something called string theory, but science doesn't approach what came before the cosmos. Science likes to measure, to construct. As far as the Creator goes, that's impossible. Space has no finite limits. And even if there was no space—no heavens, stars, or gases, just emptiness (which is inconceivable to us)—that's still the Creator. You get where I'm headed? There's no way to define what existed before Creation, but you need to believe that the Creator was there all along.

To embrace the Kabbalah, you must accept in your heart and soul that there is a Divine energy that holds the possibilities of allness and nothingness. You don't have to buy into the exact story of Creation (this is kind of hard to do if you have a working knowledge of science). Yet the story of Creation does give us a feel for what the Creator is all about.

The Creator

Kabbalists have many names for what we usually call "God." Since the Creator is infinite, more than one name makes sense—a name is confining, but the use of many names opens up many definitions.

In Hebrew prayers, the Creator is known as

Adonai (pronounced *Ah-doe-nah-ee*), or "Lord." The most observant Jews will not utter this name outside of synagogue. In the Torah, the Creator's name is written "YHVH," an unpronounceable combination of letters that is transliterated into English as "Yahweh" and also as "Jehovah." "YHVH" is the most sacred name of the Creator and as such it isn't commonly used. In Kabbalah, you'll run across more names for the Creator. This is in part because different faces of the Creator do different things. In the Tree of Life, for instance, you'll see that the Creator's "face" is called *Keter*, or "Crown." This isn't the whole Creator, just the part that interfaces with the Tree of Life.

If you consider that the Creator holds all, evil and good, allness and nothingness, you might comprehend that part of this infinite energy interacts with us in various circumstances, but it's part of a whole. If you're Christian, it's like accepting the Trinity, that the Father, Son, and Holy Spirit are the same thing in different identities.

One of the ancient names Kabbalists use for the Creator is the Hebrew phrase "Ein Sof" (rhymes with "pine loaf"). Ein Sof is the Infinite One (emphasis on "One"), all light, the Creator of all that is and all that can be, as well as all that isn't. Ein Sof is the energy of God that Abraham identified when he rebelled against idolatry. The one God, Ein Sof, is the great spiritual guide of Kabbalah. It isn't necessary that you use "Ein Sof" to invoke the name of God, but it's a phrase you'll see often.

More Names for the Creator

El Elyon — "Most High God"
Ha-Elohim — "The True God"
Avinu Malkeinu — "Our Father, Our King"
Melech Ha-Olam — "Ruler of the Universe"
Shekinah — "Divine Presence [here on earth]"

Fear of God

"Thou shalt love the Lord, thy God. . . ." That's the old-fashioned way of saying, "Respect the Creator." If you were brought up with any kind of religious training, you were probably told also to fear God, to be a "God-fearing" person. But that doesn't mean you should tremble in the presence of the Creator (although confronting an infinite force would probably reduce us to trembling).

Fear, with respect to the Creator, really means "be in awe." You don't have to interpret it as "Fear God because God's going to punish you." The Creator is simply the force that is so great we cannot conceive of it. Ein Sof is the power of all light. What can be more awe inducing?

So don't fear the Creator. Respect that unknowable, amazing source and try to add your light back to the greater good.

How We Came to Be

Here's one version of the story of Creation, which has been modified and retold over the ages.

> *Once, in the incomprehensible length of infinity, the Creator (Ein Sof) was on its own. This was the energy of all that was and all that could be. At some point in this vast, infinite existence, the Creator possessed a desire to give to something that could benefit from its energy. (The Creator wanted the pleasure of doing something generous.) To do this, the Creator formed a void, often called a Vessel. The Vessel was empty, a vacuum (which*

was still part of the Creator but was also without the Creator's energy and light). The Creator then filled the Vessel with light and was fulfilled in its desire to give. The Vessel was full.

The next part of the story is told in different ways, but the ending is always the same.

The Vessel became the light itself, but it was still contained in a finite space. It got a little too full and burst. It couldn't contain all the light that the Creator could give.

The shards of the Vessel splintered out across the great space that existed, and formed our very universe. Some found their way back to the source of the Creator, but some drifted into what is now our world. This was the moment of that line in Genesis, "And God created light." Those shards of light from the broken Vessel were the beginning of our existence. Those shards of light are fragments of the original Vessel. It's up to us, according to Kabbalah, to put those shards back together, to form the Vessel once again. Once the Vessel is intact and full, we will all be reunited in the Creator's infinite light.

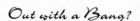

Out with a Bang?

Kabbalists currently favor the idea that the moment the Vessel broke stood literally for the big bang. The moment that "God created light" was the moment of that particular explosion in space that formed our universe. What do you think of that?

Healing the Fragments of Light

After the Vessel was shattered, the shards or fragments were covered by shells. The shells are called *Klipah (Klee-PA)*. The many fragments of light from the original Vessel are now withheld in shells and kept from shining. It's up to us to break those shells down and join the light once again with the Creator. This is the ultimate healing and the Divine intention in the teachings of Kabbalah.

How on earth do we find these shells and break them down? Let's go back to the conceptual drawing board.

The idea of the light fragments and the shells is only a way of explaining how Creation took place. The Vessel's shattering is only a story to help explain the basic idea. And the core concept of light's being captured or withheld is a way of explaining our separation from the Creator. The light that is withheld will eventually be released and returned to the Creator as good outweighs (and eventually extinguishes) evil in this existence. And good will overtake evil as we all join together to make positive choices, to participate in the greater good, to choose love over hate. What separates us from the Creator is the shells or coverings that encase the light. Your shell is within your life—your personality, your karma, your choices. As you participate in life, choosing good over evil, forgiveness over revenge, love over hate, you will contribute to the return of the light.

Kabbalah shares this belief with other spiritual practices. Light enables connection. Light is love itself, oneness with spirit, the Creator. Spiritual practice enhances your inner light, your connection to the Creator. As the light within you grows, the world feels it and is changed.

To skip ahead in our Creation story, Adam and Eve were given perfection in the Garden of Eden. Yet they could not resist temptation and chose to eat the only forbidden fruit in this plentiful, protected place. As a result of their mistake, evil entered the world and they lost their paradise. In a sense, Adam and Eve were the Vessel and they couldn't handle so much light, so much perfection. Instead of being able to cope with the Divine, they shook things up by breaking the rules.

Creation is a story about shaking up the status quo, seeking pleasure through giving as God gave to Adam and Eve, as the Creator gave to the Vessel. Making our way *back* to what was the status quo is a big job.

Why Creation?

It's possible you're wondering why the Creator got the idea to create the Vessel in the first place. Why did the Creator need to give, to share its light? What motivated the Creator?

The answer, like so much of spirit, lives within you. As beings who are supposed to make our way back to the Creator and receive and share the light, we possess a great deal of Divine knowledge in everyday life—we just don't see it.

Ever wonder why you want to have a fulfilling job,

or maybe want to start a family? Or, perhaps more basically, you feel the need to have sex? What spurred the Creator into making the Vessel and filling it with light is very much like the need to have a blast-off orgasm. It is the desire to experience pleasure. And for the Creator, pleasure is in the giving.

For us, the energy of Creation is our personal motivation. As a child, it's pure—maximize pleasure, and minimize pain. Candy over vegetables, play over chores. As we grow up, simplicity evaporates and our choices become tougher. We have to make decisions about where to go with our lives. Pleasure often takes a backseat to responsibility, obligation, and just plain old pressure.

This is not to say that you're supposed to drop everything and head to the nearest opium den. Rather, you're supposed to find the pleasure, the little piece of light (no matter how small), in whatever you do. When there is no light, no connection, no pleasure, you're in the wrong place, pal.

Creation and the desire to please and be pleased is constantly spurring you on. What to have for breakfast, what to wear, whom to talk to—even these mundane choices are part of the please-and-be-pleased dynamic. Suffering doesn't get you much. No martyrs here.

Good and Evil

Jewish folklore and Kabbalah are filled with stories about good and righteous men who are tested (Abraham with Isaac, Job with his many tests from God), as well as stories of men who aren't so righteous but learn a lesson. In Kabbalah, there is no devil, but evil plays an important role. Evil helps you be a better person.

Opportunities to open to light are often precipitated by a brush with evil. Cheating on a business deal, for instance, is considered evil. If you were to repent, however, you'd be opening to light. Holding a grudge and bearing someone ill will are evil, but apologizing and being generous enough to admit and release that grudge are opening to light.

Evil is a complex concept and will be addressed in a later chapter. Suffice it to say for now, Lucifer has no place in Kabbalah. You can't get away with saying, "The devil made me do it."

Good and Better

There isn't a soul on this earth who doesn't rub up against her own limitations, petty or important. But that's okay.

Being good isn't actually as powerful as being in the dark and opening to the light. It's a bigger deal to admit a weakness or heal a wrong than it is to be right in the first place.

Running to church, synagogue, or mosque doesn't make you a better person. Knowing when you've been wrong and allowing yourself to admit it is a much more powerful connection to light.

It's a complicated situation we're in. It's not always easy to see where the light should be shining. When in doubt, look for forgiveness within yourself, look at the shadow of the situation, and try to find out where the light is being blocked. The answer is within reach if you look inside yourself.

The next chapter will give you an idea of how you were put here on earth and the forces at work presenting you with choices.

.3.

The Tree
of Life

Trees are important symbols in many ancient spiritual
traditions. Druids worshipped in groves. Native American shamans believed trees had curative powers. Buddha found enlightenment under the bodhi tree. In
Kabbalah, the Tree of Life represents more than an ac-
tual tree. It is a map of how the Creator's energy comes
to us. Most renderings of the Tree of Life don't even
look like a tree. Some look like a crystal or a molecule;
some use concentric circles to show how the energy
emanates toward us. Many artists have interpreted the
Tree of Life. You can find numerous examples on the

Internet as well as in books about Judaism, Kabbalah, and symbols.

For our purposes, let's keep the Tree of Life as simple as possible, in "molecule" form. It's the content, not the design, that is of value.

The Tree of Life depicts the route the Creator takes to arrive at what is Created.

Structure

Although the Tree of Life can look very clean and geometric, its simplicity is deceiving. Most models show the ten "power centers" stacked in three separate columns, but when you examine the flow of energy and how the ten centers interact, you might get a better sense of how multidimensional and even loopy the Tree can be. What I refer to as power centers are also called emanations, portals that convey qualities that are essential to Creation on earth. Are they real portals? Probably not. The Tree of Life is a structure of

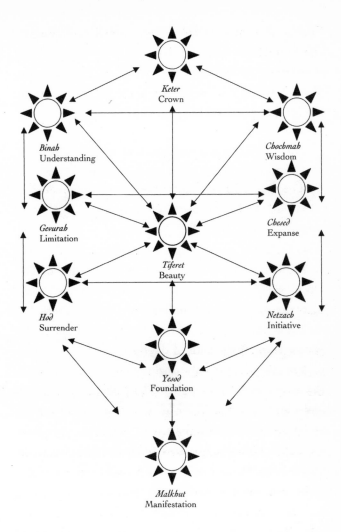

Keter
Crown

Binah
Understanding

Chochmah
Wisdom

Gevurah
Limitation

Chesed
Expanse

Tiferet
Beauty

Hod
Surrender

Netzach
Initiative

Yesod
Foundation

Malkhut
Manifestation

archetypes—it's a model, not a reality—and its symbols hold larger meaning than one word, one picture, or one point in time.

The Tree of Life is composed of energy centers called "emanations" that work together to produce life as we know it.

Kabbalists think of the Tree as upside-down. The top of the Tree, the Creator's energy, actually represents the roots. The emanations, or power centers, are the trunk and branches of the tree. The bottom, where our lives are, is the fruit of the tree.

The Tree is not only upside-down, roots to fruit, but is also read from right to left, like Hebrew. The first point is in the center at the top of the Tree. The second is lower and to the right. The third is opposite on the left side. It's not easy to get used to this when you're brought up reading left to right, so pay attention as you are guided through the Tree.

The Power Centers

The Hebrew word for these power centers is *"Sefirot,"* which means "Numbers." Each of the centers has a Hebrew name and a number, from one, the Creator's energy, to ten, the fruits of our world.

Kabbalists believe that we can't really conceive of the first power center because it occupies a spiritual plane far above our understanding. The second and third centers are also far beyond the reach of our daily consciousness, but with diligence and spiritual enlightenment, you can get closer to these Divine energies. The next six power centers, numbered four through nine, flow closer to our plane. The poor unenlightened souls (not you!) understand only number ten, *Malkhut,* which is life here on earth.

Each of the power centers represents a unique, essential element of Creation. They emanate from the Source (Ein Sof), as follows.

The Tree's Roots
1. *Keter*/Crown

The Tree's Trunk and Branches
2. *Chochmah*/Wisdom
3. *Binah*/Understanding
4. *Chesed*/Expanse
5. *Gevurah*/Limits
6. *Tiferet*/Beauty
7. *Netzach*/Initiative
8. *Hod*/Surrender
9. *Yesod*/Foundation

The Tree's Fruits
10. *Malkhut*/Earth

All ten power centers are present in you and in all aspects of your life. Every "creation," be it a birth, a new job, a new art project, even a new thought or impulse, is the product of these ten power points. How the power centers intermingle in each creation process, however, is a mystery. In certain circumstances, it may look as if one center plays a bigger role than others. Say, for instance, you've been working hard to earn a promotion, but someone else receives it. You may think that the fifth center, *Gevurah,* which imposes limitation, prevailed more than other centers. Sometimes limitation is only part of the equation, however, and it might be revealed that the delay in your promotion was beneficial, possibly a joint effort of *Netzach, Gevurah,* and *Malkhut.* It's hard to say which of the centers is pushing things, because they cooperate with one another.

Energy Flow

Naturally, it's tough to conceptualize how this Tree of Life is present in everything you are. It's only a model of how the Creator manifests our world, of how, from an inconceivable source, energies flow to our world.

Kabbalah teaches that the ten power centers of the Tree of Life are the same energy as the Creator but are used for different purposes. Here's a very simple example of how *one* source can create a number of *seemingly different* things that are still essentially the *same.*

A crystal pitcher of water is used to fill different glasses. The glasses are different shapes and colors, and the water from each glass is used for a different purpose. The water is all from the same pitcher, but the vessels look different and some water is used for nourishing a plant, some for drinking, some for cleaning, and so on. The water from the clear pitcher can take on unique colors and purposes, but it's still just water. That's how the Creator's energy flows through the Tree of Life and manifests in your life.

The Story Behind the Flow

One-Two-Three
Keter-Chochmah-Binah:
Creation-Wisdom-Understanding

Each power center has a distinct place and purpose on the Tree of Life. The first is *Keter,* "the Crown," where all emanation begins. *Keter* is unknowable. It's not exactly the same as Ein Sof, but it comes energetically closer to what we call God — too close to the infinite for us to comprehend. Kabbalists distinguish between the greater energy of all, that which is inconceivable, and *Keter,* the top of the Tree of Life, which is part of but not all of the gigantic endless energy of the Creator. This is probably why *Keter* isn't discussed much — it's hard to chop up infinity, since it has no limits. But there is a difference. *Keter* is the power center closest to the Source,

Ein Sof, and we can't touch it with our humble human consciousness.

The second center, *Chochmah,* is equated with Wisdom. *Chochmah* is all information, like an endless uncataloged library or a scattered and unlabeled laboratory. It's not organized or useful on its own; it's just there to hold all that is possible. Some scholars believe that truly understanding the nature of *Chochmah* is impossible. More modern practitioners believe that with skillful meditation, you can access this vast tier of wisdom.

Moving on from *Chochmah,* we find the third center, *Binah,* the presence of Understanding. *Binah* takes the wide-open wisdom of *Chochmah* and sorts it out. ("Binah" is also the name of the girl at the center of the story *The English Roses* by Madonna.) *Binah* is considered a feminine energy, but in truth these centers do not have gender. *Binah* is a compassionate energy but is also constricting. To impose understanding on wisdom demands sorting, which is a restrictive influence.

The next six power centers are considered closer to us and slightly easier to understand. More so than the first three energy centers, these six present opposing qualities. They act in balance with one another.

Four-Five-Six
Chesed-Gevurah-Tiferet:
Expanse-Limits-Beauty

Chesed, the fourth center, represents the quality of loving-kindness, the giving energy. From the Creator, *Chochmah* presents possibilities, *Binah* sorts them out, and *Chesed* wants to apply them or share them. *Chesed* is the desire the Creator had in wanting to share its light. *Chesed* is the nature of giving for the pleasure of giving. No return favor is necessary.

To balance *Chesed*, however, *Gevurah*, the fifth center, provides restraint. *Gevurah* has been considered by some scholars to be negative, painful limitation. *Gevurah* is the energy that separates and says, "Enough" to *Chesed*. Limitation and restraint might seem negative, but that's not really a fair assessment. At some point you have to stop receiving in order to appreciate what you have. Sometimes you have to pause in order to understand the value of something in your life. It's true that restraint is sometimes imposed on our lives, but it's pretty much always a learning experience.

After *Gevurah* comes a power center called *Tiferet*. This sixth center is a balance of *Chesed* and *Gevurah*, as well as a culmination of the higher centers. *Tiferet* is called "Splendor" by some. For our purposes, "Beauty" works just as well. In essence, *Tiferet* is what happens when extreme giving *(Chesed)* is met with temperance or limitation *(Gevurah)*. The resulting balance is beauty, something we can appreciate and absorb. *Tiferet* also holds the energy of vision, the ability to perceive how to benefit others. *Tiferet* has the vision of beauty and shares it.

Seven-Eight-Nine
Netzach-Hod-Yesod:
Initiative-Surrender-Foundation

The next three power centers take us closer to reality, the world as we know it. From "Beauty" and its vision, "Initiative" is born. *Netzach,* the seventh power center, has a purpose and the energy to stick with it. Some people call this center "Perseverance." *Netzach* is the energy of stamina and focus. It stays the course even in adversity. Therefore the vision that beauty creates can be manifested.

The eighth center, *Hod,* tempers initiative. *Hod* is "Surrender," a tricky issue and a balance to *Netzach's* will, intention, and drive. *Hod* enforces sacrifice and yielding. We can't know all that there is to know and so we can't assume that even our best intentions take into account all possibilities. *Hod* hedges the guiding force of

Netzach to keep all options open for (hopefully) the best result.

This result, by the way, is related to the power center called *Yesod*, the ninth center. This is "Foundation," the culmination of all the centers before it, the last drops of water from the pitcher. This is a processing center, the last stop before we hit our plane of existence.

Yesod is the power center that contains all prior experience. It is heritage, the transition from the past into the present. All of the power centers that come before add to *Yesod*. The foundation work of *Yesod* is then transmitted to us.

Ten
Malkhut: Our World

We are the final stop on the Tree of Life. We are the fruits of all the power centers. All the way from *Keter*, the unknowable energy, we are the manifestation of spirit.

The whole world, our perceived world, is *Malkhut*. You are *Malkhut*. And you now have some idea of how Kabbalists figure that the Creator's energy ends up in us.

Malkhut isn't a sum of all preceeding energies in some defined equation. Our reality is touched by all

Malkhut Vs Shekinah

This world we live in is considered *Malkhut* on the Tree of Life but is also known as Shekinah, "the Divine Presence," considered a feminine energy. Like the ancient goddess of the earth, Shekinah is the energy that provides the source of life for this world and its physical beauty. If you happen to run across a reference to Shekinah, it is the presence of God in the world today—a good thing.

the power centers in different ways at different times. There are obvious circumstances in which you'll feel *Gevurah*'s restraint as well as *Hod*'s insistence on yielding, and most of the other power centers, as well.

You can study each of these power centers for years, but the way to really understand and know them is through working with them in your own life. Every center has many layers and applications. The following chapter should get you started with the centers so you can use them more purposefully in your life.

Each emanation is numbered and is associated with a color (not unlike chakra colors) and a body part (because the Tree represents how spirit manifests the physical). You can also use the suggested exercises to practice accessing and deepening your understanding of each power center. Just remember, as with every other part of the Kabbalah, it's possible to find disagreement on the interpretations of each power center. The following information was culled from a number of sources and makes the most sense for the purpose of your enlightenment.

As Above, So Below

Many spiritual teachings inform us that what takes place here in our world is a reflection of the spiritual realm—this is what is meant by "As above, so below."

Working with the emanations from the Tree of Life brings about the possibility of positive outcomes on both sides—above and below. Light is enhanced. Your work with light brings us closer to the Creator. As more light is revealed, more healing takes place. The original Vessel's shards are being gathered and ultimately will be whole.

Tree-of-Life Power Centers: Symbolic and Practical Use

One
Keter–Crown

The inaccessible crown of *Keter* is something you trust more than something you consciously access. *Keter* asks you to believe, to receive, and to have faith in the guiding force of spirit.

How to Use Keter *in Your Life*
Can you do anything directly with *Keter?* No. But working with the Kabbalah, receiving and sharing light, brings you that much closer.

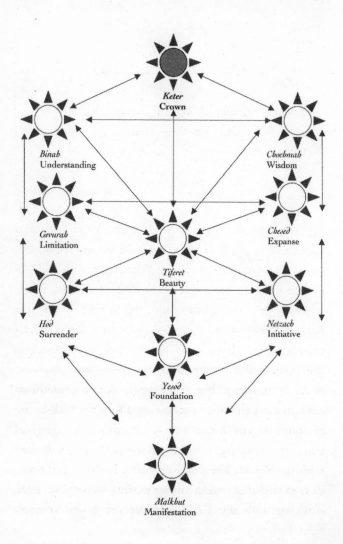

One—Keter—Crown

Energy: mystery of life/soul energy
Body point: top of head (crown)
Color: white

While *Keter* is beyond your reach, your faith and participation in your own spiritual progress connect you to this force. Prayer, meditation, acts of mercy, forgiveness, kindness, and love are all blessed acts. While anything you do, speak, think, or believe is still just part of being human, connecting in faith to *Keter* brightens your light and lifts you that much closer to the Creator.

Keep creating. Every time you initiate something, even as insignificant as inquiring about the well-being of someone you know, you're creating the energy of connection and light that the Creator itself manifested with the Vessel. There are probably hundreds of times in your day that you create or initiate something, even if it's just a thought. This is *Keter*, the desire to reach out, to please, to put energy where there was none before.

Keter is the very force of the Creator and it is embedded in all of us.

Keter *Ritual*
Receive and believe.

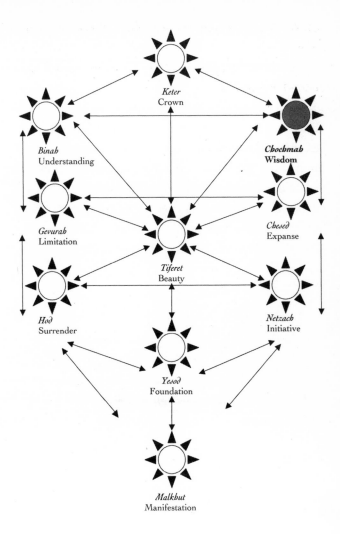

Two
Chochmah—Wisdom

Vast and infinite wisdom isn't directly available to any of us, but it is everywhere, in every part of your life. Although you may think that wisdom is something along the lines of the Pythagorean theorem or Einstein's theory of relativity, that's not really what *Chochmah* is about. This energy center is more about universal truths, spiritual knowledge, and, on our human level, intuition, insight, and perception.

Two—Chochmah—Wisdom

Energy: sudden perception, impulse to create
Body point: right brain/right temple
Color: silver

How to Use Chochmah *in Your Life*

Pay attention, look, listen, notice. That's how you hook up with *Chochmah* in your life. Rather than plod along and take every day for granted, be aware that great wisdom and direction are available to you through *Chochmah*'s universal energy.

You're already using your intuition on some level. You can feel something is about to happen, or you think about someone and boom, he calls. *Chochmah* manifests in your life everywhere, but you can increase your conscious exposure to this Divine energy by paying attention to your hunches.

Chochmah is only one step away from *Keter* and therefore it's not easily accessible. To get closer, you need to tone down distractions and tune in to the universe. That's meditation. It's not easy, but it's worth it.

If you can find a way to quiet your mind and your environment, you give yourself a chance to let *Chochmah*, the universal mind, connect with you.

Chochmah *Ritual*

On a regular basis, make quiet space in your life to open to wonder and the broader energy of wisdom. Don't look for insight; let it come to you. *Chochmah* brings you broad impressions and guides you subtly.

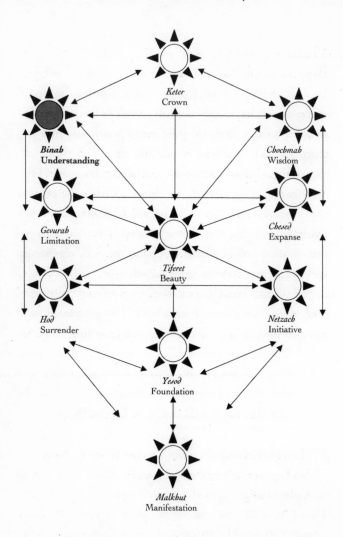

Three
Binah—Understanding

Wide-open, seemingly infinite wisdom runs into *Binah*, the gentle force of guidance. *Binah*, another remote energy center, is almost more difficult to comprehend than *Chochmah*, because of our own limits with language. *Binah* is a limiting force, a restricting energy. It's easy to fear that *Binah* hampers wisdom. But *Binah* is like a teacher who encourages you to stick to your studies, make sense of the ideas, and be patient with yourself as you grow wiser, stronger, and more capable. *Binah*'s energy gets wisdom into more useful form. Your dreams contain *Binah*'s rich offerings: encoded messages and symbols

Three—Binah—Understanding

Energy: shaping creativity, giving form to chaos
Body point: left brain/ left temple
Color: indigo

from a realm of consciousness not accessible in waking life.

How to Use Binah *in Your Life*

Binah is accessible through third-eye and dream work, undertakings that require a lot of practice. They're not for amateurs. The third eye (or psychic eye) is located in the middle of your forehead just above your eyebrows. Place your finger on it and you'll feel a slight indentation or sensitivity. Here is where your imagining, visualizing, and image conjuring are done. This is your mind's eye.

Similarly, you "view" your dreams with another kind of psychic eye in a realm that is not physical. Participating in dreams or using dreams is an access point to *Binah*.

Once you have some practice with consciously using your third eye (guided visualization is a start) or using dreams to help you out in your waking life, you are in a position to come in contact with *Binah*. *Binah* can provide images, clues, symbols, and messages through these realms.

To work with *Binah* requires faith and trust that the greater good is at work. *Binah* asks that you open to the light and be guided by events and watch for symbols sent to you in psychic/dream images. As long as you act with integrity—not selfishness, vanity, greed, fear (add your own weakness here)—*Binah* will help you get to where you want to be.

Open to light as much as you possibly can when you start to doubt or fear. *Binah* can guide you more directly when you resist it less. Remember, *Binah*'s guidance leads to your ultimate goal.

Binah communicates only indirectly, so your practice is essential to accessing this realm. If you wake from a dream with images that linger with you, or if you work with guided visualization and run into some new information or symbols, this is *Binah*. Do not be afraid—even if at first you react with fear (which is natural when dealing with a force as close to *Keter* as *Binah*). Let your fear melt to awe, opening to guidance and light. *Binah* is ultimately about understanding. And that brings light.

Binah *Ritual*

Work with your dreams. Keep a journal. Take note of symbols and intuitive messages. Try to interpret them. As you get more skillful, *Binah* gets closer.

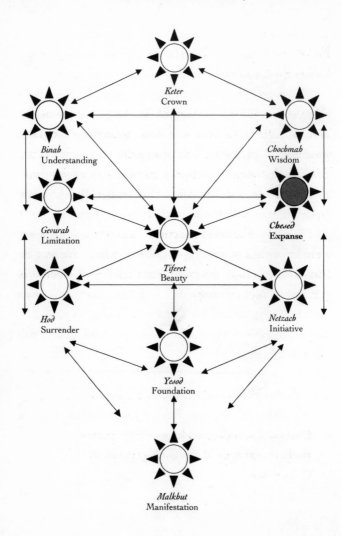

Keter
Crown

Binah
Understanding

Chochmah
Wisdom

Gevurah
Limitation

Chesed
Expanse

Tiferet
Beauty

Hod
Surrender

Netzach
Initiative

Yesod
Foundation

Malkhut
Manifestation

Four
Chesed—Expanse

From the molding influence of *Binah,* the energy in the Tree of Life flows next to *Chesed,* qualities of expansiveness, forgiveness, and unconditional love. With this fourth energy center, we come closer to our reality. *Chesed*'s properties are linked more clearly with our own practical, human experience.

Chesed is about connection. It's what makes us want to reach out and know others, to help the world. *Chesed* is wide-open, adventurous energy. It wants to get out and get moving.

Four—Chesed—Expanse

Energy: unconditional love, mercy, ecstasy
Body Point: right shoulder, right arm
Color: blue

How to Use Chesed *in Your Life*

How bad could it be to have a little adventure, ecstasy, or love? We welcome the idea of it. But using *Chesed* requires some big-time heart energy.

Chesed is associated with the Dalai Lama, Jesus Christ, Abraham, Buddha—you get it. *Chesed* is embodied in people who forgive and accept and hold both suffering and joy in their lives. Just because *Chesed* is closer to our realm doesn't mean you can become expert in its gifts. Every day has countless opportunities to use *Chesed*—and we ignore many of them.

Caught in traffic? *Chesed* would say, "Breathe through the anxiety. Forgive. Let go of the moment." Expand your tolerance. How often can you do that? How about when you're charged too much at the grocery store? Slighted by a friend? Just in a bad mood?

Chesed would have us open to light. Just being alive is enough. *Chesed* is the force that gives you opportunities to forgive and choose love over separation. These opportunities are there for you every day. It's up to you to pay attention.

Chesed *Ritual*

Take a risk without judging the outcome. Do something you haven't done before just to try it. Success isn't the point. Take a skiing lesson or try playing a musical instrument. Introduce yourself to a stranger or join a new club. Moving outside your routine or your comfort zone is beckoning the energy of *Chesed*. Make a habit of saying yes to experiences you would ordinarily shy away from.

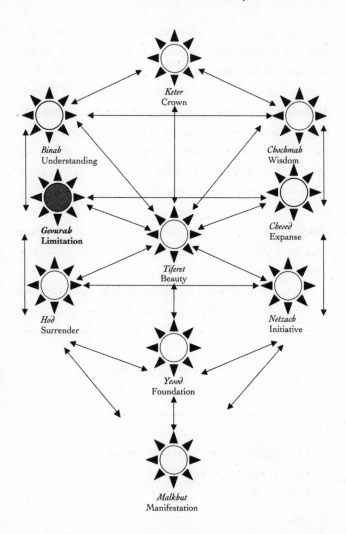

Five
Gevurah—Limitation

To balance *Chesed*'s overflowing desire to put out energy, *Gevurah* reins in energy. You might wonder why the world wouldn't do better with *Chesed* unfettered by *Gevurah*, but here's why. *Chesed* doesn't temper what it expands—it just goes for anything. Spending expands into extravagance and debt. Sunny days expand into dry earth and drought. *Chesed*'s expansiveness isn't always beneficial. You *can* have too much of a good thing.

We absolutely need the discerning force of *Gevurah* to limit expansiveness. *Gevurah* discerns, culls, and severs. At face value, *Gevurah* seems unpleasant, even

Five—Gevurah—Limitation

Energy: judgment, discipline, severance
Body point: left shoulder and arm
Color: red

evil. It's not. *Gevurah* is a counterpoint, a balance to *Chesed*. You have to stop the flow of wine in order to drink from the glass. (At least that's how I like to look at it.) *Gevurah* puts the brakes on flow so you can enjoy what you have.

How to Use Gevurah *in Your Life*

In some ways, you don't have to work to attract *Gevurah*. Though our culture encourages and expects us to expand and make progress, *Gevurah* shows up regularly to shape, redirect, or diminish that progress effectively.

There are times, however, when *Gevurah* can be called upon to fortify our efforts. Use this power center in conflicts—when you have to find the energy to say no or put a stop to something. *Gevurah* can lend you power to face foes or raise a voice of dissent.

You can access *Gevurah* through indirect means. Wearing red when you need to face conflict is always helpful. The color evokes *Gevurah* and raises your power.

You can also use the purification energy of fire to emanate the power of *Gevurah* and *symbolically* diminish obstacles or foes, as in the following prayer ritual.

Gevurah *Ritual*

On a white piece of paper, make a list of those things that stand in your way (fear is a big one, so always include that). Ask *Gevurah* to help you burn through these obstacles. Ask to find discipline, judgment, severity, limitation—whatever it is you need—to get the job done. Take this list to your sink and set it on fire. Let it burn into ash. Wash the ash away and await the energy of *Gevurah*.

Be mindful of how you react to this ritual over the next few days. Also pay attention to how things in your life might shift. Repeat as necessary.

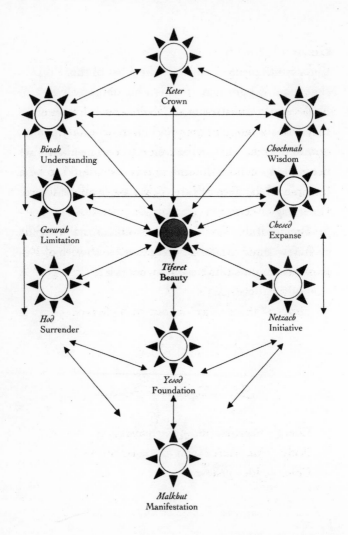

Six
Tiferet—Beauty

As *Gevurah*'s limits balance *Chesed*'s expanding energy, they find harmony in the production of beauty, splendor, and love. This is the second power center that floats in the central column and is considered to be a linchpin of the Tree of Life. *Tiferet* takes all those previous power centers and channels them into one comprehensive total. Take the unknowable *Keter,* the wilds of Wisdom and Understanding, and the forces of Expansiveness and Limitation—what would you get? A sum of great creativity.

Tiferet is the energy of love in higher purpose. It

Six—Tiferet—Beauty

Energy: heartfelt purpose, compassion
Body point: heart center and solar plexus
Color: golden yellow

has direction and discipline from Understanding and Limitation, as well as ideas and generosity from Wisdom and Expanse. This energy takes place in our lives as intention, vision, and the desire to put light and love into the world for the greater good.

How to Use Tiferet *in Your Life*

You use *Tiferet* every day, probably without even noticing. When you feel very connected to an idea, a vision, a purpose, that's *Tiferet*. When you "know in your heart" that something is right, that's *Tiferet*. Or if you "feel it in your gut," that's *Tiferet*.

What you might not know is that it's very easy to send this energy into any enterprise, idea, or relationship. Hooking into *Tiferet*'s energy is summoning your own intention and sending it out of yourself.

Take a moment to identify the two body parts associated with *Tiferet*. First, touch your heart center; you can actually feel this point on your body between your nipples in the center of your chest. Next, find your solar plexus by gently pressing your fingers upward in the center under your rib cage. You might feel a slight adrenal reaction, as if you have activated some butterflies in your stomach. It's a sensitive central power point in your body.

From these real, physical body centers, you can send energy to someone else, or even to an event or idea. This is *Tiferet* energy, the energy of vision, intention, the heart's desire. Generally this is a "greater good" force—you don't use it for negative outcomes or punishment. *Tiferet* shares light, love, and uplifting vibes.

Whenever you want to enhance something in your life, send energy through your heart and solar plexus. It strengthens and raises the possibility of making your vision a reality.

You can also use *Tiferet* to heal wounds and open to forgiveness. Sending energy to a wound or conflict can ease the pain and suffering. Love gives space for acceptance even in the most severe circumstances. For example, *Tiferet* works through the hearts of crime victims who forgive their tormentors. That's an amazing use of *Tiferet*'s energy. It's healing, open, and intent on an outcome of love.

Tiferet *Ritual*

Consciously choose something that has happened to you in the past that you need to let go of. Put yourself into a quiet, meditative state. In your mind's eye, imagine the source of this wrong. See yourself forgive it. Next, picture yourself; imagine that you are looking into your own eyes. Now forgive yourself for hanging on to pain. Give yourself comfort in your mind's eye. Open your eyes and feel the lightness of *Tiferet*'s loving-kindness.

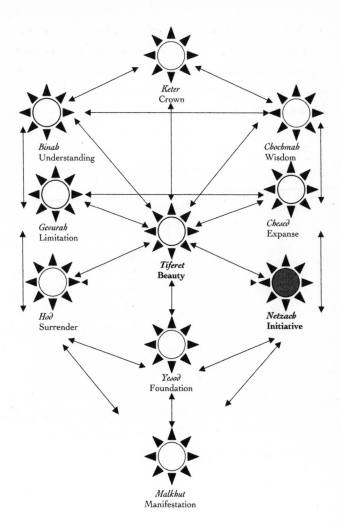

Seven
Netzach—Initiative

In response to the heartfelt purpose of *Tiferet*, *Netzach*, the seventh energy center, is ready for action. It's great to have vision, but you need more to make it real. *Netzach* is the energy to initiate the action, to bring vision into form.

Taking off from the higher emanations on the right side of the Tree—*Chochmah*, wide-open Wisdom, and *Chesed*, Expansiveness—*Netzach* gets focused. As we proceed through the Tree of Life, the energies become sharper and honed to a point. *Netzach* still emanates energy like the higher centers on that side of the Tree, but it channels this outgoing force to a purpose.

Seven—Netzach—Initiative

Energy: drive, perseverance, purpose
Body point: right hip, right leg
Color: green

How to Use Netzach *in Your Life*

Clearly, we all need this energy to get things done. Not only does *Netzach* give us the desire to do something, but it also adds to our stamina in order to keep us going under adverse conditions. It gives us the energy to form relationships, to have families, to make our personal marks on the world.

When you're feeling a little grumpy and less than excited about life, or you just need some spark to liven up, access *Netzach*. Put your best foot forward (actually, your right leg) and take a walk. Yes, get up and get out. A little physical exercise is all you need. Stop the inertia; start the initiative. *Netzach* is action — forward motion helps you get some speed going. It's easier to make something happen when you're already in motion.

Netzach *Ritual*

The process of making a mark in the world, the desire to achieve, can be accessed by planting a seed. To help an idea get planted and take root in reality, you can plant a seed and observe the process of germination, of pushing through the soil, reaching up to light. Now, that's initiative, fortitude, stamina, and growth.

By respecting and consciously observing this energy, you increase your access to *Netzach* and give strength and endurance to yourself.

Plant anything—an avocado seed, a pumpkin seed, a bean. Just watching a seed transform is an uplifting experience and opens a new light within you.

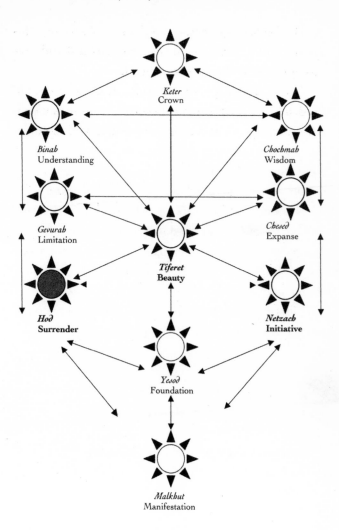

Eight
Hod—Surrender

One step forward, one step back. Sometimes that's what the Tree of Life seems to be showing us. From the seventh center of Initiative, we move to number eight, Surrender. So what are we learning here? Are we supposed to give up after we start something?

No. But *Hod* does represent knowing when to acquiesce to the greater good, the higher power. Just as *Netzach* resonates with the higher powers on the right side of the Tree, so does *Hod* connect with the left side, from *Binah,* which sorts things out, to *Gevurah,* the limiting force. We see that *Hod* echoes the theme of countering outgoing energy. *Hod* might censor the force of

Eight—Hod—Surrender

Energy: connecting, yielding, evaluating
Body point: left hip, left leg
Color: orange

Netzach and make sure it's in sync with the greater good. *Hod* opens us up to messages and information that aren't obvious—it reads higher levels of consciousness, as well as what else is going on in the world. The driving force of *Netzach* might be tempered as a result of *Hod*'s filter.

How to Use Hod in Your Life

Hod is always present, whispering doubts, urging you to take into account others' needs and feelings, ever sensing what is good for the whole and not just for you. You can easily access *Hod* by asking questions, being aware of your motives, and respecting the truth, whatever it may be. There are times when what you want isn't what you get. *Hod* will tell you when that's going to happen—and you'll know it ahead of time.

Hod isn't about diminishing your goals or your initiative from *Netzach*. It's there only to make you aware of the environment in which you push yourself. Is what you want good for others, too? Remember, Kabbalah is about receiving and sharing your light, not just opening to light and holding on to it. *Hod* sometimes gives you clues as to when it's better to relinquish what you want because it's just not best for all involved.

Hod *Ritual*

Keep a journal of curious colors, symbols, people, or communications that you might encounter. Look for clues and cues. That's how *Hod* comes to you. To open more to *Hod*, test your power of connection. Meditate on your goal and open to symbols, impressions, or feelings that come to you. If you're not goal focused, simply ask *Hod* to bring you signs in your life, and record what you observe. *Hod* is subtle but constantly whispering. Your journal will reflect *Hod*'s message.

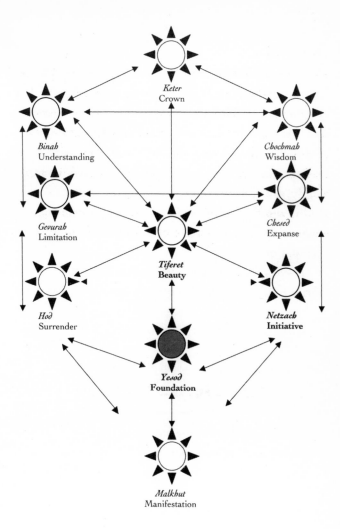

Keter
Crown

Binah
Understanding

Chochmah
Wisdom

Gevurah
Limitation

Chesed
Expanse

Tiferet
Beauty

Hod
Surrender

Netzach
Initiative

Yesod
Foundation

Malkhut
Manifestation

Nine
Yesod—Foundation

Yesod, the ninth emanation, is another center point in the Tree of Life. It floats beneath *Tiferet*, Beauty, and well below the Crown of *Keter*. *Yesod* is another point of culmination, integrating all the energy centers that came before it to produce one portal that speaks directly to our own physical realm. The previous eight emanations all channel through *Yesod*, and form a foundation of spiritual energy that feeds our reality.

Yesod is the stopping point before Divine energy is borne into our reality. We don't actually know how

Nine—Yesod—Foundation

Energy: passing on, sex, death
Body point: genitals, womb
Color: purple

much gets edited by *Yesod*. In a divine screening process, *Yesod* filters what energy makes it to us and what doesn't. It's a go/no-go point.

How to Use Yesod *in Your Life*

Yesod is the emanation closest to us, other than our own reality. It's the magical moment when spirit is channeled toward us. You can relate to it by recalling the energy of orgasm, when you lose your conscious self in ecstasy, detached from physical reality. This is a brief interface with the Divine—a glimpse of *Yesod*.

Yesod is related to the sexual organs because it holds forces that join to make our reality. It creates the foundation for life itself.

Being the foundation, *Yesod* also represents your genetic, spiritual, and cultural heritage. You are the product of all that came before you on every level. This includes your prior incarnations as well as your DNA.

To work with *Yesod*, you need to integrate all that came before. Be clear about your background, your beliefs, your physical being. To shun or deny who you are is to repress your future. You don't have to carry on traditions you don't like or observe a religion that means nothing to you, but you have to own that it is part of you. Anytime you deny a part of yourself, your background, or your beliefs, you diminish the energy of *Yesod* and thus dim the light available to you.

We all do this, by the way. You're not alone in the desire to wipe unpleasantness or embarrassment out of your past. It just won't go away. The best way to release the grip of inherited pain or problems is simply to forgive.

Yesod is based on all heritage, the good and the bad. That is true for all of us. Painful as it might be to admit less than perfect histories, you'll suffer more if you don't.

Be your own watchdog. If you find yourself sidestepping truth, look carefully at your motive. Once you realize that your shame or fear is causing you to lie or deny, let it go. Forgive yourself for what came before and open to what can happen now.

Do you pretend to be something you're not?

Do you cover up family secrets?

Do you inflate your past accomplishments?

There are numerous ways you can deny your past. Ultimately, they don't work. You only dim your own light.

Yesod *Ritual*

Make a list of your known ancestors and their histories. Do some research on your family tree, or if you
can't uncover anything, research your cultural heritage. You'll find some interesting information about
those who came before you. You'll be inspired by
them, as *Yesod* urges you to bring the fruits of their
work into your world.

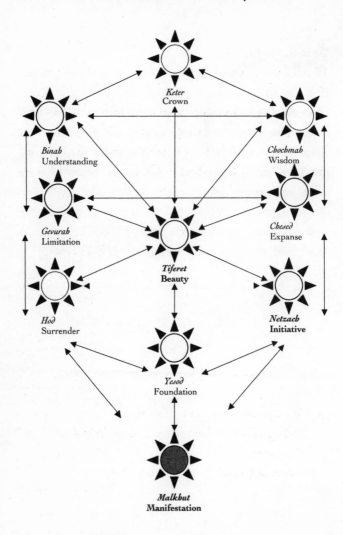

Ten
Malkhut—Manifestation

Here we are at the end of the line: *Malkhut* is the result of the previous nine energy centers. This is you, your life, where you live, the whole thing. Everything we have here is a product of the previous emanations. Thus, there isn't one single quality that describes *Malkhut*. It's everything around us, the physical, emotional, creative, passionate, and spiritual energies we have here on earth. *Malkhut* is what is manifested.

Ten—Malkhut—Manifestation

Energy: experience, life, breath
Body point: feet, base of the sacrum (the root
    chakra)
Color: red, black

How to Use Malkhut *in Your Life*

Malkhut is your chance to open to the light and to share it. Receive, believe, and share what you have. Best of all, you use *Malkhut* just by breathing. So hey, you're already an expert. Yet there's still room for improvement. Being truly alive is being conscious of every moment. Being aware of your motives, being open with your heart and forgiveness, clearly living each moment, no matter how mundane—this is the purest *Malkhut*.

In Orthodox Judaism, there are prayers for almost every part of daily life, from sunrise thanks for the new day to the blessing over each meal. No doubt these prayers originated as a way to connect each moment to the Creator and to experience wonder and respect for life. Unfortunately, most of us don't have the time or desire to think about each moment and make it count to its fullest. Our lives are littered with tasks and necessities—work, grocery shopping, cleaning, paying bills. Yes, every single thing is an opportunity for a spiritual moment, but let's face it: most of us can't live like that.

Rather than focus on every minute as a way to connect to the Creator, try opening to light and sharing it. Give a moment to reflection when you begin a new task, before you leave the house, or when you make dinner. Open yourself to light and feel the energy infuse your body. Take this feeling with you as you move through your day. It's not easy maintaining the light, but it's worth inviting it into your day. Each time you open to light, you open to the possibility of sharing light and living in joy.

Joy is what life is all about. Find the joy in your daily life. Share that joy. Even if your life has pain, take a moment to just open to light. Any connection to light, no matter how small or fleeting, can heal.

To use *Malkhut* is to live with an open heart, acceptance, inspiration, and the ability to recognize fear as a veil that dims the light. As you confront and diminish fear, you open to more light. The less you fear, the more you connect to spirit. This brings you closer to evolving beyond this realm of *Malkhut*.

Malkhut *Ritual*

Write the name of each power center on a small slip of paper. Place the slips of paper in a bowl. In the morning, pick one slip and read the name of the power center you chose. Take a moment to reflect on its meaning before you get your day going. At night, take a moment to think about how that emanation played a role in your day. Put the paper back into the bowl. Repeat the process. You will soon begin to see how the Tree of Life speaks to you on a personal level.

The Significance of Numbers and Letters

Deciphering Codes

Kabbalah is a practice that encourages paying attention to yourself, your motives, and your surroundings. As you learned from the Tree of Life, it's up to you to make the most of your relationship to the Creator and to open to light as much as possible. You can go further by examining details. This requires working with the symbols and clues that surround you.

You've already been asked to pay attention to subtleties in your dreams and meditations. The emanations of *Binah* (Understanding) and *Hod* (Surrender) provide you with symbols and connections to higher consciousness, but to get to them you have to meditate and practice honing your skills at symbolic interpretation.

Kabbalists also use more direct means of deciphering the Creator's guidance, through gematria, Jewish numerology, which explains the meaning of Hebrew letters with respect to numerical values.

You may already be familiar with Western numerology, in which the numbers one through nine are assigned meanings and you can reduce any combination of numbers to find its singular meaning. You can also equate each letter of the alphabet with a number and thus ascertain the numerological value of words. These values are considered powerful influencers or predictors of future events.

Meaning of Numbers

Numbers had important meaning to the ancients. The Bible is filled with numerical references, which is one reason Kabbalists are intrigued by their meanings. Here are some of the numbers studied in Kabbalah for their prominence and meaning in history and the Bible.

1

One is the most important number, referring to the Creator, who is One. One also represents marriage, how two souls unite as one.

2

There are two tablets of the Ten Commandments, and two brothers, Cain and Abel, to represent opposing forces. Two is balance, as well as equal powers fighting against each other.

3

Three are the fathers of Israel—Abraham, Isaac, and Jacob—as well as the sons of Noah. Three is a very common biblical number and has become part of many superstitions over time, such as the belief that deaths occur in threes, or that spitting three times averts the evil eye. Three is not, however, a Holy Trinity in Kabbalah.

4

Aside from the four matriarchs, Sarah, Rebekah, Rachel, and Leah, there are four questions to be answered as well as four cups of wine to be consumed in the Passover seder. Four is a number of ripeness and plenty.

Western Numerology

Take any combination of numerals. Add them together until you reduce the number of digits to one.

Example: Your address is 5682 West Maple Street.

Add 5 + 6 + 8 + 2 = 21; 2 + 1 = 3. The numerical value of the address is 3, growth and positive energy.

Take it a step further and interpret the words of the address through the numeric place of each letter.

A	B	C	D	E	F	G	H	I	J	K	L	M	N
1	2	3	4	5	6	7	8	9	10	11	12	13	14

O	P	Q	R	S	T	U	V	W	X	Y	Z
15	16	17	18	19	20	21	22	23	24	25	26

w e s t M a p l e S t r e e t
23 + 5 + 19 + 20 + 13 + 1 + 16 + 12 + 5 + 19 + 20 +
18 + 5 + 5 + 20 = 201, then
2 + 0 + 1 = 3.

The entire numerical value for the address 5682
West Maple Street is 3 + 3 = 6.

Six is the number of prosperity, harmony, and
happiness. This should be a happy home!

Number	Meaning
1	solitude, initiation
2	partnership, couples, balance
3	growth, positive energy, the Trinity
4	equilibrium, balance, stasis
5	conflict, discomfort, a creative state
6	harmony, prosperity, happiness
7	risk, change, exploration
8	rewards, satisfaction
9	the ending, "3 3s," closure

5

Five are the Books of Moses in the Torah. Five fingers are spread when hands are held up in blessing. There are said to be five levels to the soul. Five is a more mystical and mysterious number than the previous numbers.

6

The Star of David is a six-pointed star, and six is the number of days the Creator used to make the world. Six is a number that represents work and endurance.

7

The seventh day the Creator rested and this is the Sabbath. Seven has many mystical connotations and is found throughout the Bible. Add the three patriarchs and the four matriarchs and you get seven. It's a number that is used in many rituals, from weddings to funerals — a number that symbolizes completion.

8

After the completion of seven, eight is almost a new beginning. A baby boy is eight days old on the day of his bris, or ritual circumcision. The miracle of Chanukah involved a rededication of the Temple when the one-day supply of lamp oil somehow lasted for eight days. Eight is a pivotal number.

10

Obviously there are ten Commandments, as well as ten energy centers *(Sefirot)* on the Tree of Life. There are ten Jewish high holy days, from Rosh Hashanah to Yom Kippur.

12

There are twelve months in the lunar year, twelve tribes of Israel, and twelve signs of the zodiac, and Jacob had twelve sons.

13

This is the age of maturity in the Jewish religion. At thirteen a boy has a bar mitzvah (and a girl has a bat mitzvah). There are also thirteen Principles of Faith.

18

This is the numerical value of the word "life" in Hebrew, something we'll cover in the next section.

20

This is the age men are considered old enough to fight, so it is a number that represents maturity on a level higher than the number thirteen.

40

The maximum human life span is supposed to be three times forty. The first forty years are to get to solid maturity (remember, only men over forty used to be allowed to study the Kabbalah), the second forty are old age, and the last forty are for exceptional individuals (Moses, for example, died at 120). There are many instances of the number forty in the Bible, including the forty days and forty nights of the Flood.

70

There are many mentions of seventy in the Bible and therefore the number is considered important. Ten is the number of emanations on the Tree of Life and seven is the number of days in the week that the Creator made the world (and rested). Ten times the number of Creation is considered very powerful.

No, I didn't forget the number nine or fourteen or fifteen; I'm just mentioning the most important numbers culled from the Torah and other ancient teachings. They don't gel with Western numerology, so don't be tempted to mix the two. Numbers in the Kabbalah are used for more complicated, less personal analysis.

Who Knows One?

These are the lyrics to a song sung at Passover (the original song is in Hebrew) that gives children a brief lesson in numbers as symbols. Lyrics have shifted over time and some versions of the song are a bit different, but "one" is always the same.

The song poses a question for each number, and the answer always recites each response going back to the number one, as in the song "The Twelve Days of Christmas."

QUESTION: Who knows what one is? ANSWER: I know what one is: one is God our Father in heaven and on earth.

QUESTION: Who knows what two is? ANSWER: I know what two is: two tablets of the Law. CHORUS: One is God our Father in heaven and on earth.

QUESTION: Who knows what three is? ANSWER: I know what three is: three are the patriarchs. CHORUS: Two tablets of the Law, one is God our Father in heaven and on earth.

QUESTION: Who knows what four is? ANSWER: I know what four is: the four mothers of Israel. CHORUS: Three are the patriarchs, two tablets of the Law, one is God our Father in heaven and on earth.

QUESTION: Who knows what five is? ANSWER: I know what five is: the five Books of Moses. CHORUS: Four mothers of Israel, three . . .

QUESTION: Who knows what six is? ANSWER: I know what six is: the six days to make the world. CHORUS: Five Books of Moses, four . . .

QUESTION: Who knows what seven is? ANSWER: I know what seven is: the seven days of every week. CHORUS: Six days to make the world, five . . .

QUESTION: Who knows what eight is? ANSWER: I know what eight is: eight days before circumcision. CHORUS: Seven days of every week, six . . .

QUESTION: Who knows what nine is? ANSWER: I know what nine is: the nine months of childbearing. CHORUS: Eight days before circumcision, seven . . .

QUESTION: Who knows what ten is? ANSWER: I know what ten is: ten are the Commandments. CHORUS: Nine months of childbearing, eight . . .

QUESTION: Who knows what eleven is? AN-SWER: I know what eleven is: the eleven stars up in the sky [in Joseph's dream, Gen. 37.9]. CHO-RUS: Ten are the Commandments, nine . . .

QUESTION: Who knows what twelve is? ANSWER: I know what twelve is: the twelve tribes of Israel. CHORUS: Eleven stars, ten . . .

QUESTION: Who knows what thirteen is? AN-SWER: I know what thirteen is: the thirteen attrib-utes of God [Exod. 34.6–7]. CHORUS: Twelve tribes of Israel . . .

Kabbalistic Numerology: Gematria

Gematria is the practice of assigning numbers to He-brew letters and, much as in Western numerology, re-ducing a word to a numerical value. But gematria goes on to find and identify other words with the same value and make connections between them. These nu-merical values and connections have sacred meaning that has been studied for hundreds if not thousands of years (of course there is disagreement about when and how gematria came into use). There are many permutations of gematria, some with complex encoding rules. For our purposes, we'll explore the simplest and arguably most often used method.

Hebrew letters, derived from ancient Aramaic, are unfamiliar to most English-speaking people. As you recall, Hebrew is written and read from right to left, already a severe departure from our training. Further, Hebrew uses vowels differently. While there are two letters whose names sound like the vowel *A* (aleph and ayin), they are silent letters. There are no real vowels in Hebrew but rather vowel sounds (guiding pronunciation) that are written as dots—like our periods, but appearing in different places around letters—or small lines underneath words. Since you won't be reading Hebrew, you don't need to know these sounds, but if you happen to see written Hebrew and notice these symbols, you'll know what they are.

Let's face it. It's tough to learn Hebrew and absorb its mystical associations with numbers. But as someone who wants to know a little bit about Kabbalah, it's not a bad idea for you to become familiar with the Hebrew alphabet. This chapter presents a chart that illustrates Hebrew letters and the numeric values assigned to them. Vowel sounds don't have separate values, so they're not included.

The Hebrew Alphabet and Its Numerical Values

מ ט	ח	ז	ו	ה	ד	ג	ב	א
Tet	Chet	Zayin	Vav	He	Dalet	Gimel	Bet	Aleph
(T)	(Ch)	(Z)	(V/O/U)	(H)	(D)	(G)	(B/V)	(Silent)
9	8	7	6	5	4	3	2	1

ס	ן	נ	ם	מ	ל	ך	כ	י
Samech	Nun	Nun	Mem	Mem	Lamed	Khaf	Kaf	Yod
(S)	(N)	(N)	(M)	(M)	(L)	(Kh)	(K/Kh)	(Y)
60	50		40		30	20		10

ת	ש	ר	ק	ץ	צ	ף	פ	ע
Tav	Shin	Resh	Qof	Tzade	Tzade	Fe	Pe	Ayin
(T/S)	(Sh/S)	(R)	(Q)	(Tz)	(Tz)	(F)	(P/F)	(Silent)
400	300	200	100	90		80		70

א
Aleph
(Silent)

NUMERICAL VALUE: 1

Aleph is the first letter of the Hebrew alphabet. It might seem like the letter *A*, but it has no sound on its own. This is one of those silent letters, which take on a sound only when a vowel is applied to them.

MEANING OF ALEPH:

Initiation. One is the beginning. The Hebrew word for the Creator, "Ein Sof," begins with the letter aleph.

As a silent letter, aleph is malleable in its pronunciation depending on which vowel is applied. As the beginning of the alphabet and a symbol for initiation, aleph is the force of birth. It is energy to make things happen.

ב

Bet

(B/V)

NUMERICAL VALUE: 2

Bet is the second letter of the alphabet and can sound like a *B* or a *V.*

MEANING OF BET:

Receptiveness. The Vessel that holds light, life, possibility.

Bet stands for receiving, partnership, and duality. The number two gives a reflection to the single number one. This reflection is a symmetrical partner to one. Bet balances aleph and allows its initiation process to get to the next level.

Bet is the first letter in the word *"baruch,"* or "blessed."

ג

Gimel

(G)

NUMERICAL VALUE: 3

Gimel is the third letter of the alphabet and sounds like a hard *G*.

MEANING OF GIMEL:

The process of growth. The fruits of creative energy.

Like the number three is in Western numerology, gimel is the product of one and two, the partnership of preceding numbers that gives birth to the offspring. Gimel develops energy into reality. It is the next phase of the cycle of life.

Gimel is the first letter in the word *"gilgul,"* "reincarnation."

ד

Dalet
(D)

NUMERICAL VALUE: 4

Dalet is the fourth letter of the alphabet and is pronounced like the letter *D*.

MEANING OF DALET:

Wholeness. Readiness for spiritual opening. A door.

Dalet is a letter that integrates the previous energies. It provides a platform for exploration, a threshold between your current reality and the expansiveness of the spiritual world. Dalet is the unity of you as a being and your internal "soul" that connects to the Creator.

Dalet is the first letter in the word *"Drosh,"* Hebrew for "examining, searching."

ה

He

(H)

NUMERICAL VALUE: 5

He (sounds like "hey") is the fifth letter of the alphabet and is pronounced like the letter *H*.

MEANING OF HE:

Higher consciousness, access to enlightenment.

After you've passed through the threshold of dalet, you're now in the realm of Divine wisdom. He is the meditative space that reveals messages to you through symbols, feelings, and psychic reception. He stands for the revelation that comes to you in an open state of consciousness.

He begins the word *"Hayyot,"* the Hebrew term for higher angels.

ו

Vav
(V/O/U)

NUMERICAL VALUE: 6

Vav is the sixth letter of the Hebrew alphabet and sounds like the letter *V*.

MEANING OF VAV:

Assessment, a pause to contain what has come before.

Vav is the number six, as in the six days to make the world and the six sides of a physical object (top, bottom, right, left, back, front). All that has come before is evaluated in order to understand it and use it more effectively. Vav is a letter that resonates well in your daily life—it can clarify and connect what is available to you.

Vav is the first letter in the Hebrew word for "confession," *"vidui."*

ז

Zayin

(Z)

NUMERICAL VALUE: 7

Zayin is the seventh letter of the Hebrew alphabet and sounds like the letter *Z*.

MEANING OF ZAYIN:

Pause, rest, conclusion.

On the seventh day God rested after creating the world. This seventh day is an acknowledgment that time can be empty of work. Zayin is a reference to the space on the cosmic continuum that we call time. There is no such thing as time for the Creator. Zayin gives us pause to consider that concept, to connect with spiritual matters, and to stop working.

Zayin begins the word "Zohar," the main book of Kabbalah.

ח

Chet

(Ch)

NUMERICAL VALUE: 8

Chet is the eighth letter of the Hebrew alphabet
and is pronounced with a sound not found in English.
The *ch* comes from the back of the throat, like a cat
hissing, like a rolling *K* sound.

MEANING OF CHET:
Health, life force.

As the first letter in the word *"chai,"* Hebrew for "life,"
the letter chet is lucky. Chet stands for strength and
stamina. It's also the first letter in the word
"Chochmah," the name of the second energy center,
which means "Wisdom." Chet connects spiritual energy with real-life vitality. Wear a *"chai"* for health and
life energy.

Chet is also the first letter of the word "chutzpah," or
"audacity."

ט
Tet
(T)

NUMERICAL VALUE: 9

Tet is the ninth letter of the Hebrew alphabet and is pronounced like a *T*.

MEANING OF TET:

Intention, goodness, sharing.

Tet is the first letter of an important word, *"tov,"* meaning *"good"* in Hebrew. Tet is the culmination of all the numbers that come before and directs them into a purpose. Tet is the resolve to make a difference, to use what you know and what you can create to bring light into the world.

Tet is also the first letter in the word "Torah," the first five books of the Bible.

י

Yod

(Y)

NUMERICAL VALUE: 10

Yod is the tenth letter of the Hebrew alphabet and is pronounced like a *Y*.

MEANING OF YOD:

Yod is a spiritual moment, a connection to the full Divine energy from the Tree of Life.

Yod is the only letter in the whole alphabet to float above the line. It's a mystical letter, one that is associated with God's hand in our lives. Yod gathers emanations from the Tree of Life, shifting their powers and rebalancing them to pour into our reality. Yod is what can change your day, your attitude, your life, in one Divine stroke.

Yod is the first letter of the word "Yisroel," or "Israel."

ך   כ
Khaf   Kaf
(Kh)   *(K/Kh)*

NUMERICAL VALUE: 20

Kaf is the eleventh letter of the Hebrew alphabet and it sounds like the letter *K*. Kaf is the first letter that can be written two ways. The long-stemmed khaf is used only when it's the last letter of a word.

MEANING OF KAF:

Unity of heart and mind, intention and initiative.

Kaf combines two qualities, spiritual ideal and real ability to use it. Some Kabbalists consider the energy of kaf a delicate aperture, a site of *Keter*'s opening as it approaches us. To connect to the energy of kaf requires skillful meditative practice.

Kaf is the first letter in the word *"Keter,"* the "Crown" energy center on the Tree of Life.

ל

Lamed

(L)

NUMERICAL VALUE: 30

Lamed is the twelfth letter of the Hebrew alphabet and sounds like the letter *L*.

MEANING OF LAMED:

Learning and teaching. Your ability to know Divine knowledge.

Lamed is the tallest Hebrew letter and has always been associated with sharing or learning information. The most harmonic point of lamed is when you learn something new and it *feels* right. When you learn in your heart and you know in your mind, this is lamed.

Lamed begins the Hebrew number lamed-vav, or thirty-six, the number of hidden saints the Kabbalists believe are here on earth, keeping us together.

מ   ם
Mem   Mem
(M)   (M)

NUMERICAL VALUE: 40

Mem is the thirteenth letter of the Hebrew alphabet and like kaf is written two ways. The second mem (on the left) is used only at the end of words. Mem is the sound of *M* in English.

MEANING OF MEM:
Messengers, mystery.

Mem is about the deep unknown, the infinite well of creativity and energy that we simply don't have the capability to understand. As the value forty, mem recalls the forty years the Israelites wandered in the wilderness, and the forty days and nights of the Great Flood. You can interpret mem as the holder of wisdom that can send messengers and angels to guide us in the face of the unknown.

Mem is the first letter in the word *"mazel,"* which means "luck/fate."

ן   נ
Nun   Nun
(N)   *(N)*

NUMERICAL VALUE: 50

Nun is the fourteenth letter of the Hebrew alphabet. It also has a final-letter form: the stemmed nun on the left is used only at the end of words. Nun sounds like the letter *N*.

MEANING OF NUN:
Faith.

Nun is a straightforward letter. It stands for faith, for the trust you put in the Creator, for that which you know to be true even in the hardest times. Nun is how you know that you'll be taken care of, that you can rely on the Creator to see you through each day. Nun is that leap you take in a risk. Even if you fall, you can get back up.

Nun is the first letter in the Hebrew word *"neshama,"* meaning the soul's connection to higher awareness.

ס

Samech
(S)

NUMERICAL VALUE: 60

Samech (remember that *ch* makes the rolling *K* sound of the letter chet) is the fifteenth letter of the Hebrew alphabet and is the sound of the letter *S*.

MEANING OF SAMECH:

Protection and support.

Some Kabbalists assert that the circle suggested by the way the letter samech is written emphasizes the protective energy of this letter. Samech is the energy of the Tree of Life that is in everything here on earth. Samech is Divine Presence and therefore protective. It is the wholeness of the Creator in all that is reality.

Samech is the first letter in *"Sefirot,"* the Hebrew name of the emanations on the Tree of Life.

ע

Ayin
(Silent)

NUMERICAL VALUE: 70

Ayin is the sixteenth letter of the Hebrew alphabet and it's the second silent letter. Ayin takes on sound only when a vowel sound is attached.

MEANING OF AYIN:
Comprehension, insight.

Ayin is your ability to witness, integrate, and use perceptions that are "under the current" of reality. Ayin is sort of your psychic ability to see and understand information that isn't being broadcast or revealed through obvious means. Kabbalah asks you to pay attention to the signs and symbols presented to you. Ayin stands for your ability to interpret that which comes to you. Ayin requires internal focus and openness at once. Discern what is meaningful.

Ayin is for *"aytz chaim,"* the "Tree of Life."

ף   פ
Fe   Pe
(F)   *(P/F)*

NUMERICAL VALUE: 80

Pe/Fe is the seventeenth letter of the alphabet and it's a complicated one. It makes the sounds of both *P* and *F*. Only fe requires a different letter to end a word, though, and the final fe is above on the left.

MEANING OF PE/FE:

Articulation, the ability to communicate through speech.

It figures that the letter that has two sounds and one final letter would stand for the quality of speech. Pe/fe also implies "Think before you speak" and suggests the power of the spoken word. Formulating what to say and how to say it is a very important part of receiving and sharing the light. Pe/fe is the inspiration to share light through words.

Pe is for *"peh,"* which means "mouth."

ץ   צ

Tzade   Tzade

(Tz)   *(Tz)*

NUMERICAL VALUE: 90

Tzade is the eighteenth letter of the Hebrew alphabet and does not have an English equivalent. The letter makes the sound of *T* and *Z* combined. Tzade also has a final-letter form that is written at the end of words.

MEANING OF TZADE:

To transform, to bring spirit into matter.

The essence of sharing light is captured in the letter tzade. Bringing spiritual energy into this plane, being conscious of the power of the Creator, and using all of your awareness to open to light and share it—that's the meaning of tzade.

It's no wonder that the Hebrew word for "charity," *"tzedakah,"* begins with this letter.

ק

Qof

(Q)

NUMERICAL VALUE: 100

Qof, pronounced *Koof,* is the nineteenth letter of
the Hebrew alphabet. It makes a sound like a *K*.

MEANING OF QOF:

To sanctify, to live everyday life with awareness of
the Creator.

Qof is the first letter of the Hebrew word "Kabbalah,"
which is why you sometimes see the spelling in English as "Qabala." Qof is about spiritual receptivity.
With respect to every moment of your life, are you
aware, open, receiving, sharing? Do you live in a state
that respects the Creator? We can't really reach the
full meaning of Qof; we can only aspire to it. It's a
guide to an evolved state of life.

Qof is for *"kabayl,"* "to receive."

ר

Resh
(R)

NUMERICAL VALUE: 200

Resh is the twentieth letter of the Hebrew alphabet and represents the sound of the letter *R*.

MEANING OF RESH:

Higher consciousness, intuition.

Another symbol of higher learning that is available through spiritual practice, resh reinforces the powers of the higher emanations of the Tree of Life *(Chochmah and Binah)*, as well as the earlier letter he. Resh has been associated with knowledge you can reach only through intuitive powers, the understanding of spirit, the innate love of God, and the belief that God is infinite, although you cannot actually understand infinity. Resh is a mystical letter that brings healing energies from the unknown into our daily lives.

Resh is for *"rofeh,"* "healer."

ש

Shin
(Sh/S)

NUMERICAL VALUE: 300

Shin is the twenty-first letter of the Hebrew alphabet. It can make either of two sounds, *Sh* or *S*.

MEANING OF SHIN:
Harmony of routine, peaceful fulfillment.

Coming toward the end of the alphabet, shin is the second-to-last letter. The story of the Hebrew alphabet begins its ending with peace and abundance, harmony and wholeness. Shin is the "allness" of your world. Everything is held in the Creator's energy. Shin means being at peace with your whole existence, not needing to separate the good and bad but accepting the entirety. Shin encourages joy because it leads you to wholeness.

Shin is for "shalom," "peace."

ת

Tav

(T/S)

NUMERICAL VALUE: 400

Tav can make the sound of the letter *T* or *S*. It is the twenty-second and last letter of the Hebrew alphabet.

MEANING OF TAV:

Renewal, redemption.

Tav is the last of the Hebrew letters and therefore carries with it the significance of what happens at the end of a cycle. Tav is the end and the beginning. Your mission in life, your purpose, is at the core of this ending and beginning. Each time you undertake a task or make an effort to create light in the world (in whatever way you choose to do that), you are in line with Tav, your purpose. Tav is the reason you're here.

Tav is for *"tikkun,"* the Hebrew word Kabbalists use to describe healing the broken Vessel. We are here to rectify the break, to bring the shards of light back to wholeness.

Using Hebrew and Gematria

Play a bit with the numbers in your life.

It might be interesting for you to figure out a rough
spelling of your name in Hebrew, then look at the

Gematria gives every Hebrew word a numerical
meaning. One fairly well-known Hebrew word,
"*chai*," translates to "life" in English.

י	ח
Yod	Chet
(Y)	*(Ch)*
10   +   8   = 18

The numerical value of "*chai*" is 18. This number is
considered a good-luck number. If you have the
number 18 in your birthday, your address, even
your phone number, it's considered a positive sign.

numbers associated with it. You can also simply find the Hebrew letters that best fit your initials and see what those numbers are. Practically anything can be evaluated for its numerical value.

My name is Barrie. I would write this in Hebrew with a bet, aleph, resh, resh, and yod (I use this for *ie*). To an English speaker, this would be like *B-A-R-R-Y*. In Hebrew it would look like this (right to left, of course).

׳	ר	ר	א	ב
Yod	Resh	Resh	Aleph	Bet
(Y)	*(R)*	*(R)*	(Silent)	*(B/V)*
10 +	200 +	200 +	1 +	2 = 413

This number reduces again (4 + 1 + 3) to 8. Eight is a number that symbolizes vitality.

If the word "Barry" were found in the Torah, Kabbalists would not reduce the number 413 any further. Instead, other words with the same value would be found and grouped together. It's the way the Torah is "deciphered" through gematria.

Scholars have attempted to interpret the entire Torah through assigning numeric value to each letter and each word. It's not a science, though. Words can be

(and have been) edited over time, thus shifting interpretation. Like Western numerology, gematria is
shaped by culture, historical context, and current ap-
plication. If you choose to study numbers through the
Hebrew alphabet, you'll develop a connection to the
letters themselves, and you'll be more open to their
powers and interpretation. Remember, some believe
that merely touching the letters of the Aramaic language of the Zohar brings a connection to the Creator.
Being comfortable with Hebrew is a step toward understanding that ancient language. With each level of

Gematria on the Internet

There's even a Web site where you can type
in your name and see what the numerical
value is and if any other Hebrew words match
it. At the time of publication, the Web site is
www.mysticalinternet.com/gematria/index.php.

knowledge, you come closer to the wisdom and powers of the Kabbalists.

More on Using the Power of Hebrew

Many people believe in the power of symbols. Good-luck charms, talismans, hex signs, you name it — every culture has them. Hebrew letters offer you another form of power, luck, or protection.

Now that you have a reference guide to the letters and their meanings, you can use them. To increase your intuition or inner sight, try meditating on resh or he. For health, use chet. It might seem unusual, even inconceivable, that a simple letter could possess such power and influence, but there are more than a few people who swear by it. If you're becoming involved in Kabbalah and you want to take things deeper, become acquainted with Hebrew letters and use their gifts to guide you into your light.

Gematria Is Flexible

Kabbalists have many methods to decipher words for numerical meaning, some more complex than others.

The primary goal of applying numerical meaning to the Torah was to find "secrets" about the universe and Creation. More modern Kabbalists will look beyond the Torah for numerical clues and symbols.

Although the following applications are not strictly from Kabbalah, you might find some useful insight by examining the Hebrew alphabet in connection with your own life.

Your Age

Find the letters that make your age. If you're 34, your letters are lamed-dalet. Study the meaning of these letters and see if they are signficant during this year. Or add $3 + 4 = 7$ and use the 7th letter, zayin, as your guide.

Your Birthday

Write your birthday out in the form of MM/DD. For instance, if you were born on June 17, your numbers would be 617. You can look at this as vav-aleph-zayin or you can reduce to one letter — $6 + 1 + 7 = 14$, $1 + 4 = 5$. Five is the letter he. He is your personal letter. Study its meaning in your life.

Initials

Look at the initials of your first and last names (and middle and maiden names). For instance, "Karen

Duffy Riley" is KDR, or kaf, dalet, resh. This combines to 20 + 4 + 200 = 224. This reduces to 8, or chet.

In evaluating your personal numbers, you are becoming familiar with Hebrew. Somewhere in your psyche, you've found a connection to your ancient wisdom. Take your time to see what might come up in your dreams. Pay attention to your intuitive faculty—

Some Significant Numbers

10: Commandments

18: "life" *(chai)*

36: twice "life" (often used as a number for cash gifts—36, 360, or 3600 dollars)

40: the years the Jews wandered in the desert, the number of days of the Great Flood

87: *"avodah"* (worship)

611: "Torah" and *"gemilut chasadim"* (deeds of loving-kindness)

you're likely to be opening new doors of innate wisdom.

One Last Note on Numbers

It's important to remember that this is not science. For many English names there is no Hebrew equivalent. Do your best and don't worry about getting things perfect. Gematria is really about symbols and hidden meanings. See if there's a significant presence of a number or letter in your life. Be open to its meaning and use the subtle guidance that the Creator sends you through symbols and signs.

If you prefer the purist's gematria, use the Internet to guide you to sources that will decipher the Torah's words into numbers and draw conclusions from there.

.6.

Angels,
Evil,
and the Soul's
Journey

By now you will probably agree that Kabbalah is a fairly complex body of wisdom. You won't necessarily see how each piece fits together. Every new area we explore tends to recall something from the last. For instance, the story of Creation and the Creator is echoed in the Tree of Life — the emanations start with *Keter*, the unknowable, and shift down to us in *Malkhut*. In gematria, Hebrew letters take on numeric significance and recall some qualities of emanations in the Tree of Life. Kabbalah is a layered body of teaching, not a story with progressive chapters.

Moving on from the mystery of numbers, we now look at another layer of the Creator's energy—good, bad, and how they affect you. In Kabbalah, good and bad acts are associated with angels and evil, although not necessarily *good* and evil. You're probably familiar with angels, and everyone has thought about the forces of evil. This is a big part of Kabbalah. In traditional religions, good and evil vie for your eternal soul. Kabbalah addresses this concept somewhat differently.

The Zohar is filled with stories that discuss angels, good and evil, and even the reincarnation of souls. In this chapter we'll explore basic beliefs, but since this is Kabbalah, there isn't a simple explanation for anything. For every question there are plenty of arguments.

Angels

First off, angels in Kabbalah are not the kind you see flying off buildings (in architecture), nor are they pointing arrows at hearts to create love. Angels are nonphysical beings, which means they do exist but don't have bodies. Angels probably aren't starring on

TV shows (but who knows if they shape the scripts?). Angels are messengers, here to do the Creator's work. Angels are not given free will. They are doing the bidding of the Creator and that's the end of the story. They aren't influenced by temptation, like some of us.

There are plenty of angels. In Genesis, Abraham meets angels disguised as men and treats them well. You might also remember Jacob's Ladder, the dream in which he sees angels ascending and descending a ladder (one enduring question is, if they don't have bodies, or if they do have wings, why do they need a ladder?).

Angels are working all the time doing God's work. But in Kabbalah they are not beings you can appeal to like saints. You can't pray to an angel because they're capable of doing only what they're told by the Creator. Some Kabbalists believe you can call in an angelic presence when you need help. This isn't strictly in line with what Kabbalah teaches, but there are people who claim that healing occurs or problems are alleviated when an angel is called in.

Many Jews call angels in for the celebration of Shabbat, the Sabbath, which begins Friday night at sundown. Inviting angels to a ritual adds to its energy, and any celebration is enhanced by angels' support, but they're there only to serve God.

What Is an Angel?

For those of you familiar with other metaphysical or spiritual models, angels are similar to light beings. They have an energy of their own that can transcend different dimensions. Kabbalah teaches that there is a hierarchy of angels. The most rudimentary angel is a fleeting spark of light. The most advanced angels are the following four archangels, whose names you've probably heard in a classical religious context.

Four Archangels

Gabriel — angel of strength of God, angel of fire and war

Raphael — angel of healing

Michael — angel of mercy and prayer

Uriel — angel of light of God

There are countless angels between the fleeting sparks and the four heavy hitters above. There is an angel for every place on earth, for earth itself, for the stars, for the heavens; there is an angel for every manifestation on this earth. Angels occupy a dimension that parallels ours. They have the ability to work with

Meet Your Guardian Angel

Dreams are a great place to make contact if you want to meet your guardian angel. Before you go to sleep, state aloud that you'd like your angel to come to you in dream time. Say something like "I meet my guardian angel tonight in my dreams. I wake up remembering this dream." Those of you who remember dreams easily will have no trouble recalling the details. If you're not an easy dreamer, keep trying this exercise every night before you go to sleep. It will work in a few days.

Remember that dreams are not straightforward communication. Your angel might appear to you as an animal, a flower, or any kind of symbol that shows you power or beauty or support. Angels can connect with you, but they don't have the same language. Be patient in interpreting your dreams. The more often you try, the easier it will be.

us yet remain unseen. We have to work to connect with this special realm. The more evolved you are, the better you can connect with them. Moses had many encounters with angels, both good and bad. You can try through meditation and in dreams to connect with your guardian angel, who is likely the angel closest to you and therefore most easily accessed.

Creating Angels

Kabbalah goes further in its teachings about angels. In fact, you create angels with every act in your life. Good acts, good angels. Bad acts, bad angels.

What constitutes a good act? Anything that you do as a personal choice within the greater good. For example, you're trying to work out what to do next weekend. You really want to go to a concert, and a business acquaintance just offered you a spare ticket. Here's the catch—you already promised your sister you'd drive two hours with her to go to see an art exhibit. You can't do both. Do you

A. turn down the ticket and secretly resent your sister?

   B. tell your sister about the concert and ask if
      you can reschedule?
   C. tell your sister you're sick and go to the con-
      cert?

If you picked *(B)*, you're on the right track. You don't know whether your sister is going to be generous and reschedule with you, but you give her the opportunity to choose. You also come clean about your desires and you don't manipulate anyone, as in *(C)*, or harbor a grudge that you create by your own unwillingness to tell the truth, as in *(A)*. If you do choose *(B)* and your sister says she still wants you to honor your commitment, you have another opportunity to go for the good energy. If you can open your heart, let go of the concert (it's not the last time you'll ever go to a concert), and enjoy being with your sister as you'd intended, you get more points on the side of good.

What happens if you act selfishly? You create a bad angel. In the end, Kabbalists believe that the angels argue your case before God and if you have more good than bad, you get promoted, so to speak. If you're on the deficit side, you have some work to do and back you go into another lifetime to learn. That's not to say that you won't be reincarnated if you're not a Goody Two-shoes, but you'll be more advanced and won't have to learn that lesson again.

The good-angel/bad-angel story has been passed down in many forms. One such story goes something like this.

A man is grouchy, tired, and feeling overburdened by life's demands. He seeks advice from his rabbi. The rabbi makes him wait, and while waiting, the man falls asleep. He dreams he sees wagons full of angels come together to a town square. There are wagons of dark angels and wagons of white angels. As a dark angel steps forward, so does a white one. They unite into a gray angel and disappear. The man sees that there are many more dark angels. He realizes that the angels are his own deeds in life. The dark angels are his lies and cheating, his bad attitude, and his selfish choices. The white angels are his charity, his kindness, and the sacrifices he made for others' well-being. Uh-oh. He needs to drum up more white angels or the dark angels will win and the judgment will not be favorable.

The man wakes up from his dream and leaves the rabbi's house without seeing him. Instead of asking God for easier times, the man now hopes for more difficulties. Why? He needs to act with kindness and charity. He needs to create more white angels.

This story is a Kabbalistic form of "When you're given lemons, make lemonade." When bad things happen or you don't get your own way, if you can open your heart to compassion instead of shutting it down in anger, you're going to create more light.

Is it possible to be good all the time? Of course not. You're human. The Creator gave you free will. You have choices to make. No one can get through even a day without some form of challenge. No one can act out of compassion every moment. It is something we aspire to, not something we achieve—at least not yet.

Dark Angels and the Role of Evil

Kabbalah has many ways to explain angels, both white and dark. Not all the stories agree (I hope you're getting used to this), but in the end the principle is the same: dark angels and evil are part of the Creator. Remember, the Creator holds the infinite universe.

Kabbalah teaches that the Creator filled the Vessel with light and that the Vessel burst. The shards of light that must be brought back together are encapsulated in shells or husks, called *Klipot* in Hebrew. Our good deeds, our compassion, scratch away at this

An Ancient Form of an Evil Gal

Lilith was Adam's first wife, created from dust just as Adam was. She demanded equal treatment (the story says she didn't want him to be on top when they made love but rather beside her). When Adam tried to overpower her, she evoked the name of God and ran away to the sea and mated with demons. Lilith became the queen of evil and now torments men (she's a troublemaker who tempts men with sex) as well as hunts and eats children.

The story of Lilith can be traced back to other ancient societies. Lilith is a reinterpretation of primitive goddesses that represented the dark side and unknown forces (including childbirth), like Innana, Hecate, and Kali. The shadow of the goddess is creative mystery, but since the dark also harbors fear, anger, and spite, these goddesses are often seen for only their bad qualities.

The interpretation of Lilith and the evil feminine is particularly harsh in strict Judaism and

Kabbalah, due in part to the fact that many Kabbalistic texts were written during the Middle Ages, when women were still considered inferior beings, yet dangerous, corrupting influences.

covering and reveal more light. *"Klipah"* (the singular of *Klipot*) has come to be understood as evil. Anything that shields light or keeps light from being shared is not good.

Some Kabbalists believe that the *Klipah* is a fallen angel, a female angel who was created along with the sea monsters mentioned in Genesis. The *Klipah* is feminine and most often hidden. The Zohar says the *Klipah* hides in the form of others. She is not actually mentioned by name because that would empower her, although she is also known as Lilith.

It might be disturbing to you that evil is feminine, but if you look at the Bible, you can see that women do take a fair amount of blame for tempting and corrupting men. You don't have to accept that evil is feminine, but knowing about it makes some of the more conservative Kabbalah teachings easier to understand. Now you know why the purists believe you have to be a man to study Kabbalah.

Another story of the *Klipah*, the fallen angel, shows that she was simply a victim of her own desires. Although it contradicts the fact that angels don't have free will, this story claims that the *Klipah* resisted her assignment as a creature of the sea and instead wanted to be closer to the Creator. She tried to get close by flying up to the heavens but got tossed back to the sea. When Adam and Eve got expelled from Eden, the *Klipah* was released from the sea. At that point the story says the *Klipah* multiplied (coupling with Cain), and the evils of the world expanded. As in the Lilith story, the *Klipah* supposedly hunts for children (innocents who are closer to God) and kills them.

Does the *Klipah* remind you of Pandora? It's a familiar archetype of the evil or dangerous feminine. While Pandora's curiosity compelled her to open the forbidden box that contained all the ills of the world, it is the *Klipah*'s desire, *selfish* desire, that compels her to act. She hunts for children because they are close to God—like the angels or Adam and Eve. She longs to be close to them or to possess them. She wants what they have. Her desire is to find light through someone else (to devour light, actually) rather than open herself up and heal so that she can have light all on her own.

She's not entirely doomed, though. Kabbalah believes that *Klipah* can be healed. Anything can be healed when it opens to the light.

Evil and the Evil Eye

The *Klipah*'s energy is the root of the evil eye. You've probably heard of people who are superstitious about the evil eye, or maybe you've seen someone react strangely or utter weird words when something good happens. The evil eye isn't a gaze that turns you into cinders. It's the eye of envy, the stare of someone who wants what you have. It is begrudging of happiness and health. It doesn't want you to have anything good, and if you do, the evil eye might take it away.

God forbid something good happen. Then it can be taken away.

The *Klipah*'s desire to have the light of the Creator is envy. She wants what she can't (or doesn't) have — and if she can't have it, neither can you. The old — and I do mean ancient — superstition about the evil eye is to never mention anything good you might have. If you do happen to mention something lucky or fortunate, you might want to spit (this is a favorite of the old Eastern Europeans) or say *"Kinehora"* (pronounced *kin-a-horra*), a Yiddish mutation of the Hebrew phrase *"kayn aynhoreh,"* which loosely means "no evil eye."

"How's your job?" "Great, *kinehora*." "I love your shoes, *kinehora*." (I'm not envying them; I just like them.)

The Red-String Dilemma

If you've seen those red string bracelets on various celebrities, you might have heard that they are associated with Kabbalah. There's even a book about them. The red string bracelets are supposed to protect the wearer from the evil eye. Now here's the dilemma. When you see a celebrity wearing something, does it make you want it, too? And what if you don't have the money to pay for what she's wearing? What if you don't have twenty-six dollars for a piece of red string any more than you have a thousand dollars for the latest handbag? It's going to provoke envy. "Why can't I have that?" Madonna gets a red string, but she's so rich, she can afford as many as she wants—uh-oh. Is that bracelet going to protect her from the evil eye or attract it!

The red string has become a status symbol, a fashion statement. There is no power in that.

There are many scholarly voices who call the whole red string bracelet phenomenon fake Kabbalah. It's not in the Zohar or in any other teachings. So beware of wanting one of those strings. It could be *Klipah*—and who needs that?

Evil in Us

We all have our own little *Klipot* to deal with. Not that
we want to eat children, but we want things for purely
selfish reasons. We want a better car, a bigger home,
designer clothes, better vacations, more money, etc.
We all have the desire for things; we often mistake the
yearning for spiritual completion with the desire for
"stuff." You can't consume enough to feel fulfilled. Ultimately you learn that "stuff" won't make you feel
better—connection to light is what you need.

Be aware of your motivations. If you realize that a
great car or a nice new outfit isn't going to fill you with
light, getting it won't be so important. The Zohar has
stories about enlightened beings who go from rags to
riches and back to rags. Look at Moses. He was aban-
doned by his mother, then raised in a palace; he was
the hero who led his people through the desert, but he
never got to the Holy Land. And he was able to stay
on course and faithful to God in every condition.

Your responsibility is to open to as much light as
possible. Don't succumb to envy or desire. Explore
your feelings. Know that if something valuable or re-
warding comes to you, it's fine—you don't have to

give it back. But if you lose it or it leaves, that's fine, too. You can't take it with you.

The Evil Side of the Tree of Life

Many Kabbalists agree that the ten energy centers from the Tree of Life hold not only the productive forces of the Creator but also the darker side. The "evil" that comes with each emanation can be considered as follows.

Energy Center	Positive/Good	Negative/Evil
Keter	This emanation holds both good and evil.	
Chochmah	Wisdom	Confusion/ignorance
Binah	Understanding	Fear
Chesed	Expanse	Conditional love
Gevurah	Limitation	Anger/punishment
Tiferet	Beauty	Narcissism
Netzach	Initiative	Sloth
Hod	Surrender	Lying, deceit
Yesod	Foundation	Resisting change
Malkhut	Manifestation	Hoarding

If you feel yourself blocked or unable to access your usual internal buoyancy, check out the darker aspect of these emanations. You'll probably be able to self-diagnose the cause of your less-than-sparkly disposition. All too often, even when we know what's bothering or blocking us, we don't do anything about it. Instead of wallowing in your darkness, start scraping away that shell. Concentrate on the positive side of the energy center. Feeling angry? Open to the message of limitation that *Gevurah* is offering. Feeling less than motivated? Let *Netzach* get you going with some initiative—a simple walk outside would help. Revisiting the gifts and powers of the energy of the Tree of Life is an excellent way to treat a little *Klipah*.

The Greater Purpose of Evil

Most Kabbalists recognize that evil was created alongside good. Some philosophize that we need evil in order to choose good—why would we ever evolve without pain, challenge, difficulty? Since evil is part of the Creator, how can evil work against us?

These issues are juicy topics for theologians and Kabbalists. You will probably have to come to terms with your own definition of evil eventually, but to start off, consider more recent thinking.

Evil is what covers light. But a covering can be removed. Evil is something that can be changed, transformed. You can shift things around in your own lifetime and help the *Klipah* in your life fall away; you can choose to let light come through. Choices that result in more light bring you closer to the Creator.

Evil may be prevalent, but the situation is not hopeless. Nor are we necessarily headed for Armageddon. Satan's showdown with the righteous doesn't actually happen within the Kabbalistic model. Instead, we struggle with evil every day.

The *Klipah*, evil, of daily life happens when instead of opening your heart to acceptance, compassion, and forgiveness, you let things like fear, anger, malice, and envy rule your actions.

There have been times (and many think we're still in a time) when evil has been overwhelming. World

War II is a great example. One of the greatest evils is the leader who appeals to the good in people for the purpose of executing his evil intentions. Hitler was able to convince a lot of people to follow his lead into darkness. Today, many fundamentalists both here and abroad proclaim that their own beliefs are the only way to respect God. You know better than that.

Is Evil Winning?

Do you believe that there is more evil than good in the world? In your personal world?

Evil (in its broadest interpretation) is where there is no light—where fear, anger, and malice lurk, or where you turn your back on doing the right thing. Every day you have choices—will you act (or react) by sharing light or by withholding light?

In Kabbalah, your individual actions are very important. You aren't acting solely on your own. Each time you open to light and share it, you help heal the Vessel. It's easy to see how overwhelming evil can be—war, famine, anger, greed—but harder to see the light. Keep your focus on the light and you'll be more likely to share it.

God Is Great, God Is Good

Ein Sof holds everything, including good and evil. God is the part of Ein Sof we address our prayers to—the redeeming and compassionate side, without the evil.

What Is Good?

In Kabbalah, life isn't solely about being good and living by the rules. You actually evolve more by recognizing where you went wrong and being able to fix it, if only by being sorry.

Recognizing how you can open to and share the light is more powerful than simply leading a good life. It's almost as though you're supposed to approach temptation, succumb, then repent (really repent). This isn't a ticket to go and rob a bank or eat like a glutton, but to notice that every day you are confronted by choices. It's the little situations that add up and make a difference.

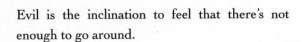

Evil is the inclination to feel that there's not enough to go around.

One of the most important aspects of opening to light is the ability to let go of what you have. It's a central component of Buddhism (all is transient), and here it is in the Kabbalah, too. Everything goes. Nothing is permanent. Even your life is going to end.

In that regard, when someone asks to borrow your car, do you say yes or no? If someone comes to your house for dinner but never reciprocates the invitation, do you hold a grudge or let it go? Evil isn't just being bad; it's withholding your generosity.

This is a gray area, of course. There are times when it is not appropriate to be generous. Sometimes people need to be resourceful and solve their own problems. Sometimes you're not willing to take a risk with your property.

Examine your motives, though. It's important that you realize where your decision comes from. Are you hoarding your fortune and not giving to charity? Are you feeling smug that you can own three cars and not even use them? Evil wins when you make your decisions without your heart.

A Word on Words

The spoken word has enormous power. Kabbalists believe that uttering the name of God is impossible (the unpronounceable name "YHVH") and that saying the true name of the *Klipah* is not allowed (if it is known). On the positive side, the prayer called the Shema, the most ancient Jewish prayer, is said aloud by Jews of every denomination and is a powerful commitment to faith. Its message is simple: the Creator is One.

> Shema Yisroel Adonai Eloheinu Adonai Echad. *Hear, O Israel, the Lord, our God, the Lord is One.*

Given the emphasis on the power of the spoken word, you can imagine how important it is to be aware of what you say and how detrimental it is to pass along criticism, negativity, gossip, or lies.

Speaking ill of someone or gossiping is literally passing along or creating evil. What makes you want to put someone else down or to share the story of another's misfortune is often the need to feel better about yourself. Of course, it's not always possible to sidestep criticism, especially when you're asked to comment directly. It's better to tell the truth than to lie, but it's important not to be unnecessarily harsh or judgmental. You're allowed to reprove but not to insult. Watch your words and don't talk about other people unkindly.

Living with the lessons of the Kabbalah takes a lot of patience and mindfulness. In this age of electronic communication, cell phones, and constant socializing, you're seriously put to the test.

The Good of Being Good: Your Soul's Path

Kabbalah very much believes in the journey of the soul through reincarnation. This is generally not something that is taught in Jewish Sunday school, but it is absolutely essential in Kabbalah.

First, it's important to know that in Kabbalah, there is no death. Your body might go, but your soul is eternal. And it's the soul that's important.

Your body is your own shell, or *Klipah*. Not that your body is evil, but it is restrictive. Your soul is encased in the shell of your body, and as a result, you naturally mistake the limitations of the body as the limitations of the soul. Not so.

Your soul is part of the Creator. While your body will return to the earth (ashes to ashes, dust to dust), your soul is not trashed when your body is dead. You get recycled, hopefully with more light to your credit.

Remember that the angels you've created in your life, the light that you've drawn in and shared, carry with you into the afterlife, where you are judged. Judgment is not supposed to be very harsh, so not to worry about little sins and mistakes. The places where you turned the corner and chose to open your heart should pull you through the judgment.

Kabbalah believes you come back to another life after judgment. Traditional Judaism doesn't. Kabbalah teaches that you get an afterlife rest stop of about a year (some Kabbalists say you're reviewing your life and you might get tortured, but that's a grim and medieval take on the overall idea). Eventually you're sent back for another appropriate lifetime specially conceived to allow you to work out whatever issues you have left. There is a Divine design in the process of your soul's return, but no one can say with certainty exactly how that works.

Returning to a new lifetime gives you a chance to evolve, as well as helps the world raise more sparks of light. Most souls have to come back; many others want to, simply to help the world connect with light.

That is the reason that you keep coming back. We're all supposed to be helping the Vessel back to wholeness. The goal is to put that Vessel back together and boom, it's time for paradise. As more light is raised, more *Klipah* is healed, and the Vessel gets closer to whole.

When the Vessel is whole, all the dead will be resurrected, and everyone on earth will be invited to paradise. (That's everyone — not just Jews or those who study Kabbalah.) If that Vessel is whole, there is no more evil and every soul gets admitted to heaven. Kabbalah teaches that this coming together of light should take place in about 237 years, give or take a few years. This is only about ten generations away. We have to get moving!

It's hard to believe that we're so close to the unification of light while the world is in such disarray. But some Kabbalists believe that the *Klipah* must exert its greatest effort in order for us to understand that it's not destruction or war that works, but forgiveness and peace.

Is There a Messiah in the House?

And what about the Messiah? That's one of those topics that gets kicked around and argued about. The Messiah, a highly evolved being, is supposed to help with the transition to paradise. Maybe the Messiah comes if evil is winning; maybe the Messiah comes only when all the souls on earth are ready for that light. It's a big maybe. The main point is that you can't count on the Messiah to do all the work. You have to contribute to the healing of the world and the Vessel by opening to light, sharing light, and healing within yourself.

Some Kabbalists believe the Messiah is a real person (or a very advanced soul who takes a body) who will come specifically to unite all of our hearts and raise us into the light. Others see the Messiah as a spiritual awakening, a light that occurs within you when you come to a defining moment of spiritual understanding. At the risk of mixing religions, we may liken the Messiah's touch to what some Christians call "finding Jesus." It is an illumination of loving-kindness and compassion that changes us forever. You don't have to find Jesus to feel it, but that seems like a legitimate (if hardly Jewish) access to Divine energy.

A Brief Look at Jesus

If you look at Jesus' life, you'll probably agree that he was an extraordinary individual who raised a considerable amount of light (and shared it). But Kabbalah won't go so far as to call him the Messiah. Kabbalah says the world is still a work in progress and there has not yet been a Messiah. If you open your heart to light and enlightenment, you will probably be able to hold both the love of Jesus and the love of the Creator together. You don't actually have to choose and you don't have to decide which theology is right. An evolved soul will open to all possibilities and avoid saying that only one way is the right way. After all, the Creator is infinite. Can't there be infinite ways to connect to the spirit of the Creator?

At this point it's worth a brief look at Kabbalah and Christianity. If you care to look on the Internet, you'll find some pretty negative reactions in the Christian world to the current popularity of Kabbalah. This is in large part due to the fact that Kabbalists don't accept Jesus as the Messiah.

Kabbalah doesn't spend a lot of time on Jesus for the simple reason that he isn't an important figure in Judaism. Some scholars think that Jesus was a Kabbalist, though, and that he was an advanced soul whose skill was considerable.

The Purpose of Your Life

Kabbalah will not hesitate to tell you the purpose of your life. Isn't that a bold statement? You've heard the answer already, though. The purpose of your life is to raise the sparks, to open to light, and to share that light in the world. Experience joy. That is the pure and simple purpose of this lifetime and all those that have come before and have yet to come.

Your simply reading this book indicates you're participating in your purpose. You seek answers; you consider information. You don't have to accept it, but you are curious about life, spirit, and what it all means.

That is the purpose of your life.

Sure, your family, your loved ones, your job, and all the other stuff in your life are important. That's where the *Klipah* can be faced, the shells broken down, and the light brought out. Your active life, your physical life, is the playground (or obstacle course?) that provides you with countless opportunities to open to light.

You're opening right now. So go on and share it.

· 7 ·

Deeper
Explorations
of Kabbalah

In Kabbalah, everything is related. After all, we all come from one source, the Creator. That's why there is meaning in everything we come across, and that's why Kabbalists spend so much time examining symbols and codes.

So far, you've learned the basics of Kabbalah; to give you a glimpse into how Kabbalists apply and explore this knowledge, the next section will concentrate on interrelationships between the Tree of Life, numbers, letters, and other ancient symbols. Over the years, scholars have proposed different connections between the Tree of Life, letters, and numbers. As al-

ways, there's no right answer. But there's an answer
that is right for you if you're open to learning, and living within, the beliefs of Kabbalah.

The Ten Commandments and the Tree of Life

First the Creator gave Abraham a push to respect Ein
Sof, one God. That was already a big innovation. Then
Moses came along and God gave him the Ten Commandments, the beginning of Kabbalah. The Ten Commandments represent great truths of the world and keys
to living life in grace, and they are the foundation of not
just Judaism but Christianity and Islam, as well. These
basic laws are part of living with the teachings of Kabbalah.

It's an interesting exercise to revisit these ten laws
in light of the ten energy centers from the Tree of Life.

The Ten Commandments offer us a glimpse of
what we aspire to be: pure of heart, compassionate,
and spiritually correct. This is pretty much impossible
when you live on this planet.

God gave Moses these laws to help shape us into
better people. The Kabbalists give us the Tree of Life

to help us understand the road from Creator to created. Live the laws according to the Commandments and you're probably more open to the magical manifestation of the Tree of Life.

If you have a particular problem with one (or more) of the Commandments, consider the meaning of the related emanation. For instance, if you have issues with your parents (Commandment number five: honor your mother and father), examine *Gevurah*. If you are dealing with jealousy (the tenth Commandment: you shall not covet), look at *Malkhut,* what you manifest in your own life, and take responsibility. There are interesting relationships between the Commandments and the emanations. Here are some ideas to consider.

Relating Commandments to the Tree of Life

One
Emanation: Keter/*Crown*
Commandment: I am the Lord, your God.
If you're struggling with Ein Sof as the one God, you need to find that part of yourself that holds faith. This must be done before you can move on.

Two
Emanation: Chochmah/*Wisdom*
Commandment: You shall not make a
graven image.
Not bowing down to idols means that you hold the wisdom that the Creator cannot be defined in any way — artistically, poetically, musically. Wisdom is uncontainable.

Three
Emanation: Binah/*Understanding*
Commandment: You shall not take the name
of God in vain.
Respecting the name of God obliges you to hold it sacred. This requires you to restrain yourself from tossing around any of the Creator's many names, including saying, "Oh, my God." Not easy, is it?

Four
Emanation: Chesed/*Expanse*
Commandment: You shall not break the Sabbath.
Observing a day of rest is actually quite important to being open to the world around you. In our increasingly busy and demanding lives, a day of rest seems to be a luxury. But it shouldn't be.

Five
Emanation: Gevurah/*Limits*
*Commandment: You shall not dishonor
your parents.*

As hard as it can be at times to show respect to your
parents—even if they don't deserve it—you wouldn't
be here if it weren't for them. That's the bottom line,
so appreciate that basic fact of your life and show
them some sort of honor.

Six
Emanation: Tiferet/*Beauty*
Commandment: You shall not murder.
All life is beautiful in its mystery. This Commandment
isn't concerned just with human life; no life should be
taken casually. This is about intention. You need to be
mindful of the Creator's power over life and death.
Look for the beauty and splendor in every existence.

Seven
Emanation: Netzach/*Initiative*
Commandment: You shall not commit adultery.
Netzach echoes the expansiveness of *Chesed*. The darker
side of this emanation is manipulation and getting
what you want by pushing for it—conditional love.

Ignoring or breaking a commitment because of selfish desires is misusing the energy of *Netzach*.

Eight
Emanation: Hod/*Surrender*
Commandment: You shall not steal.
Letting go of control is part of *Hod*. Deceit is the dark side of *Hod*. Getting what you want by illicit or dishonest means is totally against spiritual enlightenment. Letting go and having faith is in line with the Creator's energy.

Nine
Emanation: Yesod/*Foundation*
Commandment: You shall not commit perjury.
Lying to keep the status quo or putting someone else down (particularly when it affects his or her standing in the community or in the eyes of your friends) diminishes your integrity and covers light that your ancestors have brought forth in you.

Ten
Emanation: Malkhut/*Manifestation*
Commandment: You shall not covet.
Being alive and having whatever you have should be appreciated. *Malkhut* is your world. Wasting time

wishing it were different or thinking that *things* will make you happier (rather than wisdom and light) is out of line with the intention of the Creator and this Commandment.

More on the Tree of Life

The Tree of Life is used in many ways to understand our lifetime and the way we evolve. Kabbalists use the emanations to establish a theme for each year of our lives. Modern Kabbalists associate the various emanations with numbers, Commandments, planets, even tarot cards. This is the essence of Kabbalah: researching, practicing, and breaking into new levels of understanding.

The Cycles of the Tree of Life

You'll remember that seven is an important number. The Creator made the world in seven days. In Kabbalah, seven-year cycles are used to understand life's progression. There are seven seven-year cycles before you're "complete" and then you start over. This is somewhat at odds with the number forty and the three levels of maturity defined through Moses' life, but this is Kabbalah, and there's room for more than one interpretation.

Because the first three emanations of the Tree of Life—*Keter, Chochmah,* and *Binah*—are considered above direct influence on this earthly plane, they are not used in this interpretation of life cycles.

First seven years: *Chesed*—Expansion

Ages seven to fourteen: *Gevurah*—Limitation

Ages fourteen to twenty-one: *Tiferet*—Beauty

Ages twenty-one to twenty-eight: *Netzach*—
    Initiative

Ages twenty-eight to thirty-five: *Hod*—Surrender

Ages thirty-five to forty-two: *Yesod*—Foundation

Ages forty-two to forty-nine: *Malkhut*—Manifes-
    tation

Ages forty-nine to fifty-six: *Chesed*—Expansion

And so forth

Since Kabbalah applies universal forces to the individual—that is, the Tree of Life is applied to the entire universe and to every manifestation within it—you can apply the cycle of the emanations to your home, pets, a job, even your knitting. Everything has a cycle—to everything there is a season.

Seven-year cycles are also found in astrology in the revolution of the planets Saturn and Uranus. Both of these planets are considered strong karmic influences and contribute to a shift in the focus of your life every seven years.

The Thirty-two Steps to Wisdom

The Tree of Life also holds what is considered the thirty-two steps to true wisdom. This is not a path you can jaunt along while humming a happy tune. Like most things in Kabbalah, this is a path that demands study and self-awareness. It's for you to consider and explore.

The thirty-two steps are actually created by the ten power centers themselves plus the twenty-two connections they make with one another. Moreover, the twenty-two lines that connect each emanation correspond to a Hebrew letter. This, of course, amplifies the meanings of each letter.

In another numerical model, there are five "worlds" that lead from the Creator to *Malkhut*. If you're familiar with other metaphysical teachings, you'll know these as the different realms of energy that exist separately as well as in cooperation with our existence. In

other words, these are different circuits that contribute to our existence but can operate independently,
as well.

> Steps one to ten: *Adam Kadmon,* the ancient
>   Source
> Steps eleven to thirteen: *Atziluth,* the spirit world
> Steps fourteen to eighteen: *Briah,* the realm of
>   thought
> Steps nineteen to twenty-five: *Yetzirah,* the realm
>   of consciousness
> Steps twenty-six to thirty-two: *Assiah,* our physi-
>   cal world

You can roughly apply these steps to the schematic
of the Tree of Life. In fact, this has been done in many
different ways over the years. As with the rest of
Kabbalah, there is no single accepted interpretation.
That's okay. However they're drawn, what these five
worlds and thirty-two pathways represent is how the
many energies of the Creator are proliferated and
manifested even before they get to our earthly lives.
Kabbalists have derived this concept from studying
the information provided over the centuries by rabbis,
prophets, and mystics. If you are intrigued by the five
worlds and the pathways to wisdom, you will enjoy

Twenty-two Connections of the
Ten Centers of the Tree of Life

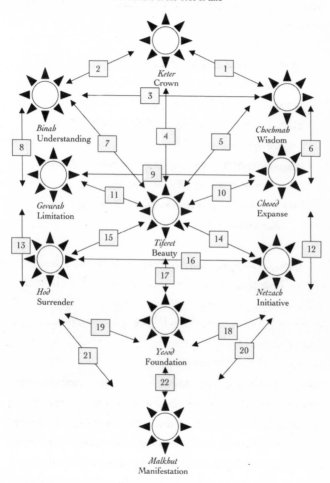

Five Dimensions of the Soul

As well as the five worlds of energy that make up our world, we all have five dimensions to our souls.

Nefesh — physical dimension *(Malkhut)*

Ruach — intellectual and emotional dimension
   (Chesed, Gevurah, Tiferet, Netzach, Hod, Yesod)

Neshama — soul's purpose *(Keter, Chochmah, Binah)*

Chayah — higher consciousness (above the Tree)

Yehidah — connection to the Creator (way above the Tree)

researching this rich topic. You will encounter Hebrew, of course, and many layers to each pathway.

Remember, scholars and commentators have assigned the energy centers and their connective lines different numbers and Hebrew letters. The numbers shown here serve merely to illustrate the pathways for you. The famous Renaissance Kabbalist Isaac Luria assigned numbers to each pathway that look very different from the "logical" arrangement here. To start with, his number one is the path from *Gevurah* to *Chesed*, which I have labeled nine. There are many more differing opinions regarding which pathway is associated with the number one and therefore the letter aleph. Suffice it to say that if you are pulled in by this kind of study, you will have a lot of theories to choose from.

Astrology, Tarot, and Kabbalah

While Kabbalists enthusiastically explored the world for meaning, they carefully avoided being considered soothsayers or fortune-tellers. In the Middle Ages, when the Zohar first appeared, the Church held strict rule over Europe, and any kind of association with divination was considered satanic. This is why you'll find less information about astrology and tarot in Kabbalah. Interpreting the stars or the archetypes on tarot cards was too dangerous for the scholars of Kabbalah.

Today, however, these topics are not as veiled from study. Some authors attribute planets and signs to each emanation of the Tree of Life.

Power Center	Planet	Sign
Keter/Crown	Neptune	Pisces
Chochmah/Wisdom	Uranus	Aquarius
Binah/Understanding	Saturn	Capricorn
Chesed/Expanse	Jupiter	Sagittarius
Gevurah/Limits	Mars	Scorpio
Tiferet/Beauty	Sun	Libra
Netzach/Initiative	Venus	Taurus/Leo
Hod/Surrender	Mercury	Gemini/Virgo
Yesod/Foundation	Moon	Cancer
Malkhut/Manifestation	Earth	Aries

There are also those who use Kabbalah in combination with the tarot. Tarot cards are an ancient method of understanding situations or divining the future, and while they may seem like a party trick more than a tool for learning, some Kabbalists see a connection between the tarot and Kabbalah.

A tarot deck is made up of seventy-eight cards. The first fifty-six cards are divided into four suits, much like modern playing cards, but instead of spades, diamonds, clubs, and hearts, the symbols are wands, coins, swords, and cups. Each suit has ten numerical cards (recall the ten emanations of the Tree of Life) and four royal cards, the prince, princess, queen, and king. These fifty-six cards are called the Minor

Arcana. The deck is completed by twenty-two symbolic cards called the Major Arcana.

Some scholars interpret the Tree of Life by painstakingly overlaying each tarot suit on the Major Arcana to understand how they work together.

For our purposes, it is more convenient and perhaps more useful to look at the twenty-two cards of the Major Arcana as they stand next to the Hebrew alphabet. The Major Arcana comprises twenty-two archetypes that depict the soul's journey from birth to death. These archetypes are quite old and probably date back to ancient times.

Letter	Tarot Card	Tarot Meaning
Aleph	Fool	Potential
Bet	Magician	Abilities
Gimel	High Priestess	Receptivity
Dalet	Empress	Feminine energy
He	Emperor	Masculine energy
Vav	Hierophant	Beliefs
Zayin	Lovers	Choices
Chet	Chariot	Ambition
Tet	Strength	Truth
Yod	Hermit	Will
Kaf	Wheel of Fortune	Destiny
Lamed	Justice	Law

Letter	Tarot Card	Tarot Meaning
Mem	Hanged Man	Vulnerability
Nun	Death	Transformation
Samech	Temperance	Conscience
Ayin	Devil	Temptation
Pe	Tower	Survival
Tzade	Star	Hope
Qof	Moon	Unconscious
Resh	Sun	Conscious
Shin	Judgment	Forgiveness
Tav	Universe	Self-awareness/actualization

As you can see, the possibilities for studying connections and relationships in the Kabbalah are endless. There are many more details, diagrams, and theories (or truths), depending on who interprets the material. Kabbalah can be analyzed by psychologists, sociologists, theologians, philosophers, astrologers — you name it, there's something for everyone.

Granted, so far this text has given you only the surface of the Kabbalah's rich resource material. You haven't seen translations from the Zohar and there are many more ancient authors and teachers who contributed to this complexly layered body of knowledge.

But what you do have so far is a great start. You

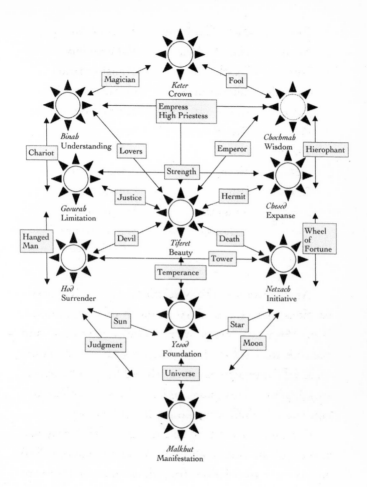

are familiar with the stepping-stones, the foundation of the Kabbalah. If you're now wondering, "Well, what do I *do* with it?" that's a good question.

Enough of the building blocks. Let's go back to reality—*your* reality—and how you can use Kabbalistic knowledge in your life.

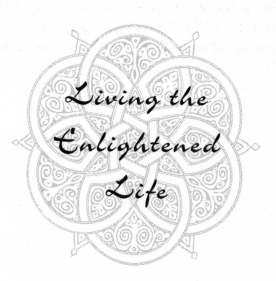

Living the
Enlightened
Life

How is it possible to use all this information to live life and open to light? It does seem a daunting task — to be aware of the energy centers in the Tree of Life, to constantly look for numbers and their meaning in words, to create white angels and live in a state of compassion and goodness. It does seem pretty much impossible.

Except you're already doing it.

Just being aware of the teachings and keeping an open heart *when you can* is living by Kabbalah. You're not expected to be a perfect being. In fact, most healing opportunities come from plain imperfection.

You're here to work with opening up, facing yourself, facing the Creator.

Kabbalah asks that you be aware of your motives and the world around you. Everything is part of the Creator. We all interrelate.

Studying the Kabbalah is different from living it. You can turn the Tree of Life upside down and inside out but not live in line with its teachings. If you want to study Hebrew, that's great. Go ahead and read the Zohar in its original Aramaic, but if you're not living with an open heart and a forgiving nature, you're not going to get real far along the road to enlightenment.

So now we'll get into tactics. These simple suggestions to lead a life within Kabbalistic teachings are not great revelations. They are guidelines you've heard your whole life. Remember, the secret is, there is no secret.

You can bury your head in books and study yourself into a frenzy of knowledge, but it's not meaningful unless you practice what you learn in your life.

Simple Steps for Receiving and Believing

The following pages are merely the basics. You might want to add your own guidelines. Just for a start, though, cruise through the next few pages and see how much pertains to your life now.

Learn

Those who study Kabbalah are perpetual students. This doesn't mean that you need to study the Zohar, but you need to be an active, participating student of life. Know that you don't know everything. Know that you can learn a lot more.

Learning isn't simply a matter of diplomas and classes. Frankly, that's not really what learning in Kabbalah means.

Learn something every day about yourself or about your relationship to the Creator. Don't be afraid to learn that you have fear. Don't be afraid to learn that you have moments of weakness.

Kabbalah is about enlightenment and advancement of the soul through personal experience and the choice and *desire* to be a better manifestation of the Creator.

Take time to learn how you make your choices. Then you'll make good ones.

Respect

"Respect" is a funny word. It evokes Aretha Franklin's passionate song or Rodney Dangerfield's humor ("I don't get no respect . . ."). But it's an important part of an enlightened life.

It's all too easy to take things for granted now: your health, job, family, relationships, and property, even this whole planet. Things come very easily to us in the Western world.

If you respect what you have, if you're mindful of who and what is in your life, you will have little cause for regret. Respect is a choice you make.

Take care of those you love and let them know they are important to you.

Keep yourself healthy. (Don't ignore your own health because you're so busy taking care of others.)

Respect money you make or that is given to you as a gift, no matter how small.

Respect all prosperity, your property, your things, your planet.

Be Generous, Part One

Generosity is a big deal if you want to live according to Kabbalah. You can look at generosity in two ways, the first being your emotional and spiritual generosity.

Living in the light and being open to receiving light demand that you not judge others or be rigid about your own rules of what's right and wrong. The only person you can fully account for is you, so it's no good measuring yourself by other people or, conversely, measuring others against yourself.

Be generous with forgiveness; be soft in your heart even when you want to be tough. A generous soul gives all it can because it isn't afraid of losing anything.

There is no judge, no court, to rule on how much forgiving is enough. According to Kabbalah, as you open to light, you advance beyond this realm and come closer to the Creator. You can afford to be generous, since others, including the Creator, have been generous with you.

Be Generous, Part Two

This is what typically comes to mind when you think about generosity. Do you serve good wines when you have company, or are you stingy? Do you count how many times someone has done you favors before you offer to help her out? Do you give your hard-earned money to those less fortunate than yourself?

This kind of practical generosity is a big part of Kabbalah. There are stories of peasants giving their last rubles to those even less fortunate and, in turn, receiving unexpected rewards. There are Bible stories about sharing crumbs and trusting the Creator to provide.

It all comes down to the basic belief that you will be provided for and that there is enough to go around. Kabbalah puts great importance on the word *"tzedakah,"* the Hebrew word for "charity." Give with your heart. Don't look for recognition or applause. Give because you are blessed to have as much as you do and there are many more people who go without.

If you want to participate in the idea of giving one-tenth of your income, please do. Various religions teach that giving ten percent of what you have is righteous. Do this if you feel it is the right thing for you.

If you are not comfortable with giving as much money to charity as the guideline of ten percent dictates, don't do it. No one can make you do it, and the Creator certainly doesn't put a black mark next to your name. You can study Kabbalah and learn to open to generosity in your own way, your own time.

It's ironic that some spiritual leaders will make demands for charity from their followers while they themselves grow rich from the proceeds.

Of course, you are not obligated to give to anyone in particular. Give to a charity of your choice, or a school, or a even a friend. Giving of yourself is the point. Trusting in abundance is the lesson. There are no rules for how to be generous. Find your comfort zone and go for it.

Put Compassion First

It's easy to lose sight of compassion, especially in a world full of contention, litigation, aggression, and defensiveness. We're told we live in a culture of blame, where we'd rather find a place to pin fault than just accept that sometimes "shit happens."

Compassion allows for that very "shit" to happen and simply lives with it. Compassion opens up the space for both the good and the bad things in life. It creates the space for everything to exist, as it emulates the Creator's infinite ability to hold both good and evil.

Let's say you had a bad day. Someone scratched your car, your favorite lunch place ran out of your must-have lunch special, you got a paper cut, and you found out your checking account was overdrawn. Then you meet a friend for dinner who complains that she can't decide whether to go to Hawaii or the Caribbean for her vacation—and she talks about it for over an hour while you contemplate using your vacation time to clean out your closets and avoid running up debt.

Do you want to reach over the table and grab your friend by her throat? Yes, you do. But you won't do that because you're a compassionate person, and you can breathe space around your rotten day (not every day is like that, after all) and let your friend be as silly as she wants to be. You know that the challenges you faced are opportunities to grow, to open up to light. So you can enjoy her dilemma over where to go, and relax. You know that by allowing her the chance to vent, you are sharing light. You don't get down on her for having different (seemingly enviable) problems. You respect her, you listen to her, and you are compassionate, even in the face of your less-than-fabulous day.

Good for you. It might sound improbable or super-human, but looking at life through the lens of a compassionate heart makes anything possible.

Take Initiative

It takes more energy to get an object (or a butt) out of an inert state than it does to increase its velocity while it's already in motion. Okay, you get it.

Get off your duff and participate in life. You're here—what else is there to do?

No more TV as anesthesia. Not that TV doesn't have its place in your life, but it's not the default activity for your body.

No more procrastination. I don't know what you're waiting for. Get up and get out there. Do some good. Meet some people and share your light. Take pleasure in the world the Creator made for you.

Acknowledge Pain and Suffering

This combines generosity, compassion, and initiative. It takes bravery and an open heart to be able to bear witness to the brutality and evil in the world, to the many children who suffer, to the people who have good intentions and hearts but who are treated with great cruelty.

You have to be able to hold the bad part of the world in your light. That will help heal it. The *Klipah* thrives in the shadows. It creates darkness. Don't let it spread. Whistle-blowers, those who protect others in perilous situations, those who stand up to bullies— these are people in touch with both the light and the dark, and they are able to hold both.

Since the Creator holds both good and evil, you're meant to aspire to the same capabilities. You can do this by seeing with compassionate eyes, being brave about standing up for the greater good, and trusting that even a small action to bring light into darkness has an effect throughout the entire universe. It does.

Exercise Free Will

Life is a long series of choices. Kabbalah asks you to choose light, choose to help raise the sparks of Creation and make that Vessel whole again. That means being conscious of your choices and choosing wisely.

Once you get on the road to enlightenment, you can't turn those lights off. Believe me, there are times when you'll wish you didn't have to be so responsible. And there will be many instances where you will act irresponsibly. You're human; it's all part of the plan.

Exercising free will isn't just about making the right choices. It's also about being sorry for those wrong turns. It is true enlightenment to know that you can be wrong, that you will be wrong, and that you will be forgiven when you are sincerely repentant.

So don't be afraid to live your life imperfectly. It's the playground the Creator gave you.

You're Never Alone

Even in your darkest times, through loss, mourning, illness, or despair, you are not alone.

Countless angels work around you all the time. The Creator's energy is manifest in everything you are and all that is around you.

This is a simple principle of Kabbalah. Even if you think you are the last being on earth, you are not alone. Ask the Creator to send you a sign.

You'll get it.

Life Is Joy

Pain, forgiveness, generosity, faith—all of this is life. And guess what? It gets the big laugh.

You are here for joy, pure and simple. That is what light is, the basic energy of the Creator. Light can come to you in the most bizarre ways—you can invite it or find it accidentally. A simple act of kindness in a random situation one day can fill you with inexplicable joy. That's the light of the Creator.

You are here to raise the light and that can only be done when you have the light within you.

Your job, your problems, your world, may seem fraught with anything *but* joy, but they offer you myriad chances to find it. Be openhearted, compassionate, generous, and forgiving, and don't be afraid to live the life you want. Don't be dim. Be alive and well and enlighten up.

Bibliography and Suggested Reading

Books

Berg, Michael. *The Way: Using the Wisdom of Kabbalah for Spiritual Transformation and Fulfillment.* Wiley & Sons, 2001.

Berg, Rav. *The Essential Zohar: The Source of Kabbalistic Wisdom.* Bell Tower Books, Crown Publishing, 2002.

Cooper, Rabbi David A. *God Is a Verb: Kabbalah and the Practice of Mystical Judaism.* Riverhead Books, 1997.

Eisenberg, Ronald L. *The JPS Guide to Jewish Traditions.* The Jewish Publication Society, 2004.

Frankiel, Tamar. *The Gift of Kabbalah: Discovering the Secrets of Heaven, Renewing Your Life on Earth*. Jewish Lights Publishing, 2001.

Hoffman, Edward. *The Heavenly Ladder: Kabbalistic Techniques for Inner Growth*. Four Worlds Press, 1985.

Hoffman, Edward. *The Hebrew Alphabet: A Mystical Journey*. Chronicle Books, 1998.

Hoffman, Edward. *Opening the Inner Gates: New Paths in Kabbalah and Psychology*. Four Worlds Press, 1998.

Hopking, C. J. M. *The Practical Kabbalah Guidebook*. Sterling Publishing, 2001.

Labowitz, Rabbi Shoni. *Miraculous Living: A Guided Journey in Kabbalah Through the Ten Gates of the Tree of Life*. Simon & Schuster, 1996.

Laitman, Rabbi Michael. *A Guide to the Hidden Wisdom of Kabbalah*. Laitman Kabbalah Publishers, 2002.

Levin, Michael. *The Complete Idiot's Guide to Jewish Spirituality and Mysticism*. Alpha Books, 2002.

Matt, Daniel C. *The Essential Kabbalah: The Heart of Jewish Mysticism*. Castle Books, 1997.

Rosten, Leo. *The Joys of Yiddish*. Pocket Books, 1970.

Sasson, Gahl, and Steve Weinstein. *A Wish Can Change Your Life: How to Use the Ancient Wisdom of Kabbalah to Make Your Dreams Come True.* Fireside Books, 2003.

Scholem, Gershom. *The Origins of the Kabbalah.* The Jewish Publication Society, 1987.

Web Sites

www.kabbalah.info
www.kabbalah.com

Advisers

Cantor Judy Greenfeld, author and teacher
Edward Hoffman, author and consultant
Elana Ponet, director of Sunday school, Yale Hillel
Rabbi James Ponet, Jewish chaplain and director, Joseph Slifka Center for Jewish Life at Yale Hillel

Photo by Tamara Schlesinger

Barrie Dolnick is a former Madison Avenue advertising executive and the author of the Simple Spells book series. She is also a high-profile consultant whose company, Executive Mystic, uses alternative information techniques, including tarot cards, astrology, meditation, and spell casting to guide clients on a successful path. For more information, log on to www.BarrieDolnick. com.